# Elaine Joli

# VACATION NATION

The Complete Guide to Timeshare,
Private Residence Clubs,
Fractionals & Destination Clubs

Contact:
Elaine Joli:  ejoli@xmission.com

ISBN:  1-4392-6137-7
ISBN-13:  9781439261378

**Visit www.VacationNationOnline.com to order 10+ copies.**

It is the author's intent to provide the reader with a model that advances understanding of the shared ownership/use industry. Examples that are used are not intended to promote or endorse any company, development, program, or service but rather to help the reader better understand the model.

To my brothers Dennis and Richard,
my sister Anita, and my friends Chip,
Jennifer and Lone for their friendship,
support, loyalty, and understanding.

# Table of Contents

# Acknowledgements

I wish to thank all the dedicated people who work tirelessly at presenting the best possible opportunities for the vacation experience in the shared ownership/use industry. These include Rob Webb, Jenny Ochtera, the folks at ARDA, Dr. Richard Ragatz, Steve Dering, Carl Berry, and Adam Wegner, as well as entrepreneurs, management, developers, resort owners, and service providers across the country. With their innovation, vision, and determination, the industry moves forward in good hands.

# Introduction

## Why Is This Book Necessary?

I can still recall our first family vacation. My parents were bold enough (or crazy enough) to take four of their five children to Niagara Falls. My youngest brother was only four and even my mother, who rivaled Marion Cunningham on *Happy Days*, agreed that it was too risky to test her maternal instincts in that way. One summer day in 1964, my dad hitched his beloved licorice-black Ford Skyliner to the large salmon can that was to be our home, and off we went.

The trip took two full weeks as we traversed the country from west to east and then back again. We saw such amazing sights, like our first look at Mount Rushmore in South Dakota, where my mother resolutely named the faces from left to right: "George Washington, Thomas Jefferson, Theodore Roosevelt, and Abraham Lincoln." We went through national parks, stopped at monuments and museums, and ate in small-town diners. We experienced mishaps and mayhem. We studied math flashcards all the way across America – my mother made learning a game, while my father remained deaf to our cries for a bathroom break.

Then we saw the falls. The breathtaking, exquisite, powerful, unbelievable fury of Mother Nature at her finest, Niagara Falls. I was eleven then, and although the images of that first vacation remain on small black-and-white photographs stored in a cigar box, my memories prevail in Technicolor. There hasn't been a family reunion without the warm nostalgic remembrances of that vacation, pouring over those small old photographs, the belly laughs, the retelling of stories (usually, the more embar-rassing the better) that have been told dozens of times, always with new embellishments but the same denials.

There are very few of us who can remember all the gifts we got or gave on holidays or for birthdays, but we all remember the vacations we've been on. Over the years I've found, that the biggest benefit to "committing" to vacations for a lifetime – and that's what vacation ownership, shared ownership, and club memberships are about – is that families plan in advance, set the dates, and *know* they are getting away.

Depending on your experience, you know a little or a lot about the shared ownership/use industry. Most of us have heard of "timeshare" at a sales presentation, while on vacation at a great resort, from folklore (both good and bad) or from a family member or friend who owns one. Some of you have wandered into a discovery gallery at a ski resort to "discover" that you could purchase "a second home without the cost or upkeep of a second home at a fraction of the price." And still others have read articles in magazines and newspapers about the most recent incarnation in the luxury travel industry, the destination club.

## The Pursuit of Happiness

Most of us have taken a vacation. Many of us take regular vacations. Many more of us would *like* to take regular vaca-tions. According to Expedia.com's seventh annual Vacation Deprivation Survey, more than 51 million Americans didn't use their vacation time in 2007, and in 2008, American workers gave up more than 460 million vacation days.[1]

Not so for Americans who own vacation ownership interests. According to the American Resort Development Association (ARDA) International Foundation, a recent study of timeshare owners found that 68.4 percent of owners report using more vacation time as a result of owning a timeshare product.[2] Why?

By purchasing a vacation ownership interest, these individuals have made a commitment to taking regular vacations with their families and friends throughout their lifetime. They have bought more than sticks and bricks or a membership plan. They are allocating funds to do the things that really matter – spending time with loved ones, sampling world culture, or making a difference in someone's life.

But this book isn't about trying to convince you that buying a share or membership in a resort property or joining a vacation club is the right thing to do. Instead, it aims to provide information that can help you make an informed decision about what is right for *your family*. It reminds you that even though you may be buying a deeded ownership or purchasing a membership in a club, is it *not* an investment that will give you a return on your money; it is *not* intended as a security, nor should anyone in this industry try to convince you that it is a "good investment," financially speaking. It is, however, an investment in how you choose to spend family time. It is an investment in experiencing your family and friends at their best, away from the stresses of everyday life, allowing you to share your wealth in a way that money alone never will. Leaf Van Boven, PhD, an assistant professor of marketing and behavioral sciences at Cornell University's Johnson Graduate School of Management in Ithaca, N.Y., studies the pursuit of life experiences as opposed to material possessions. "For a variety of reasons," Van Boven says, "investing resources in the pursuit of life experiences, doing things with other people, like vacations, tends to make people happier than pursuing material possessions."[3]

As Gandhi said, "There is more to life than increasing its speed."

My desire in writing this book is to outline some of the products the resort real estate industry has developed to accommodate the different and changing aspirations of vacationing Americans. The industry has endeavored to fill a niche with ownership and membership plans that allow many Americans to experience the types of vacations they have only dreamed about.

Along with the tantalizing and creative new wave of opportunities however, the consumer should understand and discover the nuances within each offering. Even the old, standard one-week timeshare bears little resemblance to what was offered only five years ago. Global brands like Marriott, Starwood, Hilton, Hyatt, and Wyndham have entered the industry and, by re-branding "timeshare" to "vacation ownership," have revolutionized how Americans "own" their vacations. In addition to vacationing at a favorite resort, owners now have the option of trading for a cruise vacation on a luxury liner, step up to airline counters with tickets purchased with "points" or pay for a meal in Paris the same way. Programs include excursions to exotic locales and experiential vacations like gorilla trekking in Rwanda or white-water rafting on the Colorado River.

Private residence clubs and fractionals offer shared ownership in a luxurious second home for a number of weeks per year, with the advantages of a hotel (did someone say room service?) as well as exchange opportunities, while destination clubs offer the ultimate in luxury vacation residences, experiences, and service through a country club model.

Each category will be discussed at length to illustrate the unique dimensions within the resort real estate industry.

## Three Purposes of This Book

### 1. Giving You Tools for Your Toolbox

**To present the model upon which vacation ownership, shared ownership, and club membership is based.**

Each of you has come to this book with a different set of circumstances. Some of you will have more economic resources than others. Some of you will be retired. Some of you will have a desire to reconnect with your family and are interested in finding a way to do that through the purchase of resort real estate. Some are interested in leaving their family a legacy of shared ownership in a beautiful resort property. Some of you want to be sure that when you vacation you know what accommodations you will be staying in and want to return there year after year. Others want to travel the world in luxury and have their every want and need met.

Whatever your circumstances or desire for your future vacations may be, I want to provide a model that gives you a basic understanding of the use rights, the legal framework, and the management systems in place for the three most popular options – vacation ownership, shared ownership, and club membership.

When you are in a sales office or at a sales presentation, emotion tends to take control. You are being shown beautiful pictures of exotic locations. You are imagining yourself slathering suntan oil on your body. Or you have already had a great day on the slopes, on the beach or on the golf course and you want to commit to a lifetime of this wonderful experience. In the sales office, we used to call it "being in the vapors"– meaning the euphoric state a person is in when they are having a wonderful vacationing experience. It is a prime state for selling someone something.

You could receive something in the mail that invites you to "explore the opportunity" of membership or perhaps a real estate opportunity in a fabulous resort. You look at the photographs of someone skiing deep powder or floating in pristine waters, or of a couple strolling on sugar-sand beaches with graceful palm trees providing the perfect amount of shade, and you start dreaming. There is absolutely nothing wrong with dreaming – after all, where would we be without dreams?

However, I would encourage you to take a more reasoned and "logical" approach. The Discovery Model in Chapter 1 provides a foundation for understanding each offering. It will give you the fundamentals to converse with salespeople and ask the questions that are relevant to your needs and will help you determine which product may be a good fit for you and your family.

## 2. Organizing Your Toolbox

**To outline each offering in detail using the Discovery Model.**

It is important to understand that there are several offerings in the resort real estate industry. Timeshare (or vacation ownership), and fractional interest products (which include fractionals and private residence clubs), are the major types of shared ownership opportunities. Destination clubs, the most recent entry in luxury travel, applies a country club model to its network of vacation homes. Members join a private club, pay an initiation fee and annual dues and, with that, receive access to an inventory of luxury residences and services. Each offering fills a particular niche regarding price, use rights, size of accommodations, ownership designation and lifestyle, to name just a few.

Chapter 2 is devoted to the timeshare (vacation ownership) industry. This chapter gives definition to what the model in Chapter 1 describes. It defines such things as deeds, right to use, purchase contracts, additional fees, points systems, exchange programs, use calendars, fixed weeks and floating weeks, rotation systems and club membership. Chapter 3 outlines the subtle differences between fractionals and private residence clubs – the types of ownership and use rights, space-available programs, internal and external exchange opportunities, rental opportunities, and amenity and service programs. The chapter contains examples of real-life offerings in the marketplace today and will give you an idea of the diversity that is available.

Chapter 4 defines the newest entry in the industry, the destination club. This is a relatively new concept, and most people are intrigued by the idea of a club membership that elevates vacationing to the ultra-luxury-travel level. The model has experienced some growing pains but is winning over those affluent travelers who want to stay in stunning luxury accommodations, and enjoy the ultimate in service all along the way. The chapter outlines the distinctions between non-equity and equity club membership and includes case studies that applies the Discovery Model to the two largest destination clubs.

As this industry has proved – there may be something for everyone (and every budget).

## 3. Getting the Job Done

**To help you be an informed consumer.**

When setting out to buy a new car, a new washer and dryer, a big-screen television, or even a new pair of skis, most people do some research, finding out about the specifications, the performance, the cost, and so on. When shopping for a new car, for example, you know whether it has to fit a large or small family, whether the car will be used for work or for shuttling the soccer team around, or whether you're just looking for that exotic little sports car you have always dreamed of owning. You may care about the gas mileage and whether it's time to buy a hybrid. You'll decide whether you want to purchase a pre-owned vehicle or a new car from a dealership.

Vacation ownership, shared ownership and club membership are products like so many other consumer goods. One product will be a better "fit" and fulfill your needs better than another. You should be able to determine the fit for your family for now and in the future. Families who make the right choice will benefit from something that will have lasting value for many years to come. This book will help you in your search for a lifetime of travel experiences for you and your family.

So now that you have the means and the time, take trips that really matter – spend time with loved ones, relax and refresh, or perhaps, as my parents did for our family, "expand our universe." It's time to become a vacationista!

# Prologue

## Herding Cats

Since the 1970s, when the timeshare concept first introduced the revolutionary idea of sharing resort real estate in the United States, developers have transformed, adapted, and reinvented the traditional timeshare. Respected hotel brands have entered the market and changed not only the name "timeshare" to "vacation ownership" but the whole world of timeshare by adding diversified programs that satisfy modern vacationing trends.

Twenty years later, with real estate in resort areas booming (particularly in ski resorts) and second homes unaffordable to most people, the concept of "sharing" a second home or a luxurious condominium has taken flight as fractionals and private residence clubs.

Most recently, developers saw an opportunity in another small but well-defined niche market – people who want to stay in ultra-luxury accommodations in exotic and expensive locations around the world, with the expectation of elite service for a certain amount of time every year. For those with wanderlust, the ability to travel the world was at hand. The destination club was born.

## "Aha" Moments

In the spring of 2007, I sat with Jenny Ochtera, an associate and good friend of mine. We talked about my latest obsession.

This was before I started writing this book (but after I started *thinking* about it). We had worked together for many years on fractional and residence club developments when she became COO of the most prominent timeshare and fractional sales training company in North America, winning awards and respect within the industry along the way. Jenny has since moved on to work for one of the largest vacation ownership and resort developers in the United States. I valued her opinion then and still do today, even though when I told her about the "shared ownership" theme of the book, she said with typical frankness, "I think it will be like herding cats. The categories are so disparate. Timeshare is now called vacation ownership, vacation intervals or vacation clubs, even though most of them are not really clubs but deeded ownership. Even fractionals and private residence clubs have different models. How do destination clubs fit in – they don't seem to correspond to either category?"

I nodded in agreement. It was true. I slowly got up from my chair. She happily added, "Let me know if there's anything else I can do to help."

But are the categories really as disparate as Jenny said? Indeed, timeshare, fractionals, and private residence clubs are fundamentally timeshare (as defined by state laws and regulations), definitely qualify as resort real estate, and also could be described as shared ownership. But what about destination clubs? Developers structured a club membership plan for the non-equity clubs, so there is no "ownership" per se as there is in the timeshare model, but the homes are definitely in the resort real estate and vacation category.

I had three "aha" moments. The first came during a conversation with Rob Webb, the senior hospitality partner at the law firm of Baker Hostetler, when he explained to me in layman's terms (for which I'll be forever grateful) the concept by which the term "timeshare" is defined (and which later became the basis for the model that I use).

The common thread for all categories was the concept of *use right*. In effect, all three categories – timeshare, fractional interests, and destination clubs – can be defined through a *use right* principle. Whether a large timeshare resort in Orlando, a private residence club in San Francisco, a fractional condominium in Vail, or an Italian villa in a destination club, each category operates under the *use right* principle. *Owners or club members have the right to use the property for a period of time less than a year for multiple years.*

The second "aha" moment was realizing that although *shared ownership* is the label most people in the industry use as a sort of catch-all phrase to describe the trend in the resort real estate industry, the label needs to include membership-based clubs as well. So the term *shared ownership/use resort real estate industry*, although cumbersome, is more appropriate.

The third "aha" moment was the most important. Although the Discovery Model is designed to provide a format that encompasses the three components used in the concept, equally important is how each offering is presented in the marketplace and how each accommodates certain lifestyles. At the end of the day, the differences among timeshare, fractionals, private residence clubs, and destination clubs are very stark.

# 1

## Time Travelers
## Introduction to the Discovery Model

*I was reclining in a dentist chair in Sedona, Arizona, bib strapped on, staring toward the ceiling at a poster of a tiger (a soft, snowy kitten might have been more reassuring!), when Dr. Gage walked in smiling, snapping on his latex gloves. As he pulled up a small stool, we chatted for a bit, since this was my first appointment with him. When I told him I was from Park City, Utah, he laughed and said, "We go there every year to ski." I asked him which area his family liked to ski (since there are three resorts in Park City). He replied his family always skied at the Park City Resort, because he stayed at the Marriott in Old Town. He told me that he owned a timeshare with Marriott, and loved taking his family skiing every year.*

*Naturally, this piqued my interest, and he was eager to tell me about his vacations. I asked him if he ever traveled anywhere else. He said, "We always take a ski week in Park City. We also have a membership in Lake Tahoe, but since we don't get up there regularly, we use that week to take trips around the world." He chatted happily as he worked, and I did my best to keep up my end. As he finished, he asked how the snow was for his spring ski trip to Park City. "Excellent," I replied, because it almost always is.*

*"A Remarkable Real Estate Opportunity*
*Own a second home at a fraction of the price."*
*Many folks receive this message on a postcard in their mail-*
*box or see it in an advertisement in a glossy publication.*
*The copy rhapsodizes about the benefits of owning a luxury*
*resort home without the cost and hassle of maintaining*
*a second home. The photos make you dream. The copy*
*makes you think it is possible to own a luxury home for a*
*fraction of the cost. By the time you turn the card over, it*
*almost seems like a bargain.*

*I make my way to the corner of Kearny and Market streets*
*in San Francisco on a bright, sunny day in March, to tour*
*the new Ritz-Carlton Club and Residences, San Francisco.*
*The project is built on the foundations of the original San*
*Francisco Chronicle Building. Built in 1890 by Burnham*
*and Root (the same architectural firm that designed the*
*Flatiron Building in New York), a $90-million renovation*
*has given the historic structure a new significance as the*
*Ritz-Carlton Club and Residences, San Francisco.*
    *Heidi and Courtney meet me in the lobby, and we begin*
*by viewing a two-bedroom suite on the twelfth floor.*
    *The rooms are beautifully appointed with striking dark*
*hardwood floors in the living areas, natural stone flooring*
*in the bathrooms and contemporary furnishings in the*
*living room. What strikes me most, I suppose, is the feel-*
*ing that this is a residence as opposed to a well-appointed*
*hotel suite. As Heidi chats about the amenities – gourmet*

*stainless-steel kitchen appliances, a front-loading washer/ dryer, high-speed Internet access, 24-bottle wine cooling cabinet, twice-daily housekeeping service, and imported linens plus the owner's lounge – I gaze through the window at the wide city view and think how great it would be to have this "home" to come to when I visit the famed "City by the Sea."*

*I was reading yet another article about destinations clubs, this one in the New York Times, titled "If One Vacation Home Won't Do, How About A Bunch."[1] The article described a woman whose family was thinking about buy- ing a vacation home in Jackson Hole, Wyoming, but who really couldn't imagine committing to skiing there for the next thirty years. The article continued to describe how a solution for her family was found. Laura and her hus- band became members of Exclusive Resorts, a destination club. For forty-five vacation days a year, membership was $425,000 with annual dues of $29,000. What did Laura and her husband get for that price? Laura's family can spend forty-five days at any of the club's 345 private luxury homes and avail themselves of high-end amenities and concierge service.*

The above examples explain why Jenny thought trying to put these divergent shared ownership/use offerings into one model would be like "herding cats." Dr. Gage owned a traditional timeshare; my mailbox postcard was inviting me to purchase a fractional resort property; I toured the new Ritz-Carlton Club and Private Residences, San Francisco, an urban private residence club; the article in the *New York Times* referred to a destination club. But each of these offerings *are* related to timeshare, albeit in distinct ways.

> *"I guess I should warn you: If I turn out to be particularly*
> *clear, you've probably misunderstood what I've said."*

Alan Greenspan, in a speech to the Economic Club of New York, 1988 [2]

## Begin at the Beginning – Here, Kitty, Kitty

There is one important concept to understand before we look into the details of the Discovery Model, and that is the nexus between:

*Timeshare and vacation ownership, fractionals and private residence clubs*

> ➤ All of these categories are included within the legal definition of "timeshare" varying to extent by state law. Why is that important? According to industry research, trust is a key purchase motivation cited by satisfied time-share buyers.[3] For forty years members of ARDA have worked with federal and state government officials in support of legislation to protect timeshare owners and consumers alike. As a result, in most states the consumer has a right of rescission (which varies from state to state and by company policy, but typically three to seven days) allowing the buyer to cancel a purchase contract

for any reason and to receive a refund of the purchase price. In addition, most states have laws or rules that regulate the sales and marketing of the product, protect owners' use of their timeshare interests from financial problems that may affect a developer, and provide that potential owners receive detailed information about the timeshare plan.[4]

So whenever a timeshared real estate offering is made – whether it is a one-week timeshare in Orlando, a 1/4 share fractional in Steamboat Springs, or a private residence club in Colorado, the consumer has protections under most state timeshare acts, rules, and/or laws.

➤ It is a commonly held notion that "timeshare" is simply a group of individuals who share the purchase cost of a vacation accommodation, in increments of one or several weeks per year.[5] A more precise definition comes from Rob Webb, senior hospitality partner at Baker Hostetler: *"Timeshare is a prepaid use right for less than one year occurring for multiple years in one or more vacation or leisure accommodations."*[6]

With this definition, it will be easier to see how fractionals, private residence clubs, vacation ownership/membership, and destination clubs can all be formulated into a model because the foundation of each category is defined by a use right.

*Timeshare and Destination Clubs*

➤ The link between timeshare and destination clubs is the use right principle. However, *unlike* most timeshare interests, non-equity destination clubs are *not regulated* under same state timeshare laws (equity clubs are also regulated by the SEC). Some states consider both equity and non-equity accommodation clubs subject to time-share regulations, and it is possible that states will at some point adopt laws and regulations for the purposes of specifically regulating destination clubs. But most destination clubs do not believe that their clubs are subject to timeshare regulations (in any state) and therefore typically do not comply with timeshare regulations.

*Definitions*

TIMESHARE: A prepaid use right for less than one year occurring for multiple years (depending on state law), in one or more vacation or leisure accommodations.

VACATION OWNERSHIP: Typically refers to a timeshare arrangement (that complies with underlying timeshare/condominium laws and regulations) that offers deeded ownership and related use rights for the period of time defined in the agreement, typically in one-week annual increments. Many vacation ownership companies that use "club" in their titles, use the term as a marketing term; what they are, in fact, is a variety of exchange and reservation services and vacation and travel benefits offered by the vacation ownership company to owners of deeded interest in resorts affiliated with the vacation ownership company, not a "club membership" per se.

*VACATION CLUBS*: These clubs may or may not include deeded ownership; rather, they offer membership for a period of time defined in the agreement, that allows use of accommodations (some on a priority basis) and programs.

*FRACTIONAL INTEREST*: An industry term describing deeded interest in exclusive luxury real estate that is timeshare-based, with annual (or biannual) use rights of typically more than three weeks but less than one year, offered as an alternative to second-home ownership. Two types of fractional interest real estate:

1. *FRACTIONAL* : Typically refers to deeded interest leisure real estate sold in use rights of four weeks or more, but less than whole ownership. Includes the luxury accommodation segment of the vacation home market and includes a high level of prepaid service and amenities, with an average price of less than $1,000 per square foot.

2. *PRIVATE RESIDENCE CLUB*: Often referred to as a PRC. Typically refers to a very high-end, fractional interest property, with member use only, typically with a price in excess of $1,000 per square foot.

*DESTINATION CLUB*: Destination clubs apply the country club model to vacation homes. Non-equity destination clubs do not advance any type of ownership interest to their members; rather, members join a private club and pay an initiation fee and annual dues. Members have access to a changing inventory of luxury residences around the world as well as extraordinary personal services. Equity destination club members pay an initial fee and annual dues, and hold an equity position in the club.

## The Vacation Experience

Now that the cats have been "rounded up," what makes the industry purr? The catnip that attracts developers to this industry is the opportunity to provide a foundation for the vacation experience. By providing accommodations, services and amenities for large and small families, for families who love to explore or just love to ski, for families with modest or sizable disposable incomes, for those that have one week or twelve weeks a year to vacation, developers want to provide the best starting point for their owners'/members' vacation experience. And the great ones do just that.

## THE DISCOVERY MODEL

One of my favorite programs on NPR is *Car Talk*. Tom and Ray Magliozzi are "Click and Clack, the Tappet Brothers," and I think they are two of the funniest people on the planet. The program is an interactive talk show where ordinary folks call in with their car problems.

One caller phoned in recently with a problem regarding teaching her sons to drive a "stick shift." She complained that over and over again, her sons could not make the transition from releasing the clutch and accelerating without "hopping" down the road, feeling totally ridiculous and then stalling out. Naturally, Click and Clack shared their own stories about the mishaps and hysteria involved with teaching kids the basics of the "stick."

But here's where it got interesting. Ray told the woman to drive to an empty parking lot for the driving lesson. When the boy was behind the wheel, once again eager to master the stick shift, she should not allow her son to step on the gas at all. He was to sit behind the wheel and only work the clutch, letting it out very slowly to make the car move forward, not using the gas pedal at all. When the boy could work the clutch to make the car move forward but not release it enough to stall the car, then, Ray suggested, he was ready to use the gas pedal. Ray asserted that mastering the basics of releasing the clutch would be the foundation for adding the gas.

In a way, I am going to keep you in the "parking lot" for a few minutes while you familiarize yourself with the basics of the Discovery Model – the "clutch" of shared ownership/use. After you master the model, you're off on the vacation owner-ship/use highway, where, frankly, there is no speed limit.

The Discovery Model is quite straightforward. It includes three components that are congruent in all the categories: *use right, use system,* and *use management plan.* Although each plan – whether it is a traditional timeshare, vacation owner-ship, fractional, private residence club, or destination club – is unique to a particular developer, the most common options are outlined in the Discovery Model.

> *"Willie, why do you use a gun when robbing banks?"*
> *"I find the best way to get my point across is to use*
> *a few well-chosen words – and visual aids."*

Willie Sutton, famous bank robber

## The Short of It

The model is made up of three pillars and is as simple as A-B-C. The first pillar is the A *use right,* or the amount of time a person has the right to use the property; for example, one week or five weeks. The second is B *use system,* or the legal framework/ regime and policies for the use right; for example, a deeded interest or a leasehold interest. The third is C *use management plan,* the procedures and plans that manage how the system is going to work; for example, if the program will be in points or fixed weeks.

Developers in the shared ownership/use industry use these three pillars as a foundation for their offering of resort real estate, and then they release it to the public. With the help of this model, it should be easier to understand any shared ownership/use vacation opportunity presented.

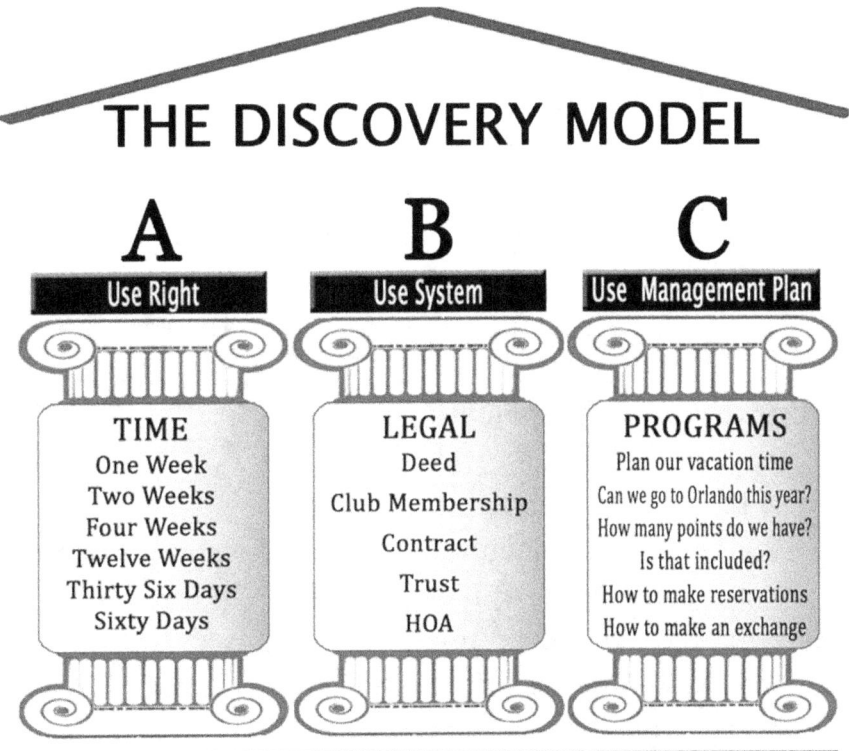

## The Long of It

**A** **Use Right:** A term used to describe the amount of "time" you have to use shared accommodations each year. Use rights for vacation ownership include one week (traditional time-share), several weeks (fractionals and private residence clubs), or a variable number of days (for destination clubs and vacation clubs).

**B** **Use System**: The use system defines how the use right is legally structured and the policies that govern that use.

## Ownership (can be)

1) Fee simple deeded
2) Deed to trust
3) Right-to-use (RTU)
4) Leasehold
5) Club membership (trust mechanism/internal exchange mechanism)

## Program documents (can include)

1) Purchase contract
2) Disclosure document (public offering statement)
3) Declaration of timeshare plan
4) Estimated operating budget
5) Covenants, conditions and restrictions (CC&Rs)
6) Management agreement rules and regulations
7) Exchange affiliate agreement
8) Physical description
9) Public report
10) Membership application
11) Club membership agreements

**C** **Use Management Plan**: The use management plan is the action plan for the policies outlined in the use system. For example, your contract will state that you have a deeded interest and are responsible for annual dues. The contract may also state the permitted percentage of annual increase to those dues. The use management plan will tell you how and when the annual dues are to be paid, whether property tax is included or not, how notification of an increase in dues is required, and how to make reservations for your use(s).

To use another example; you have a deeded interest for a 1/4 share in unit 123 in a condo. The use management plan will include the reservation policies, a *procedure* for reserving the twelve weeks in the condo. Your use right may be one week every month based on a perpetual rotating calendar that allows you to have access, over time, to every week of the year, or it may feature elements of "first come, first served."

## Use Management Plan (can include)

1) *Usage methods*
   - Fixed
   - Floating/flex
   - Rotating
   - Split week
   - Biannual
   - Points
2) *Reservation Methods*
   - Set calendar
   - Rotating calendar
   - Rotating priority
   - Space available
   - Advance reservations
   - Holiday/peak season reservations
3) *Fees*
4) *Value Added Programs*
5) *Vacation Exchange Programs*
   - Internal exchange
   - Affiliate partner exchange (External exchange)

### Examples of How the Model Works
Let's take a hypothetical example for illustrative purposes.

*John and Ellen Smith are interested in purchasing a time-share. They love vacationing in Sedona, Arizona, and since his parents live there, and they every year in February or March, they thought it would be nice to stay in a great resort rather than the mixed bag of hotel or motel rooms. Staying with his parents is out of the question (for oh so many reasons). So they take a tour with sales representative at a timeshare resort.*

*The residences are large, with furnishings that reflect the Southwest, and include a large balcony with great views of the spectacular red rock. The amenities include an owner's club with fitness center, two swimming pools, and a fire pit.*

*The salesperson tells John and Ellen about the vacation ownership family of resorts they could exchange weeks with as well as the external exchange membership and that their deeded week will be transferred into points.*

*John and Ellen decide they can purchase a week in the mid-season, since their vacation time is fairly flexible. The salesperson outlines the different programs that they can participate in: the "Happy Family Internal Exchange Program," the "External Exchange Program," the "Lifestyles Program," and the "The Perks Program." Each of these programs is designed to enhance membership but may include additional fees.*

For our purposes, let's just outline the basics of what's being offered, following the model.

### **A** Use Right
One week in "silver season"

### **B** Use System
Deeded interest (1/52 share in unit #432)
Purchase contract
Disclosure document
Declaration
Estimated operating budget
CC&Rs
Management rules and regulations
Exchange affiliate agreement
Physical description of the property

### **C** Use Management Plan
The interest has been converted to reflect 1400 points
Guidelines and rules, including:

1) Procedures for reservations: points and use calendar that outlines which dates are available for each resort, calendar for "silver" season
2) Procedures for using the Happy Family Internal Exchange Program (no additional fees)
3) Procedures for the External Exchange Program (including additional fees)
4) Procedures for using the Lifestyles Program (no additional fees)
5) Procedures for using the Perks Program (including additional fees)

Let's look at another hypothetical example, this one illustrating the Discovery Model with a fractional offering.

*Chad and Barbara Jones live in Denver with their three daughters. Their favorite place to ski in the winter is Mount Werner in Steamboat Springs, Colorado. In their sixth season they discovered that the non-skiing seasons in the Yampa Valley offered an abundance of warm weather activities they enjoyed such as hiking, mountain biking, and horseback riding. They were tired of renting random condominiums and hotel rooms, and thought that owning a second home would be great. After looking at the real estate market, they found that the second homes that suited them were too expensive and the cost and time to maintain the home was going to be prohibitive to their lifestyle. So they considered "sharing" a property. They found a ski-in, ski-out location of a 1/4 share resort property, which gave them twelve weeks a year in a three-bedroom unit. The residence had a state-of-the art kitchen, two master suites, a large, comfortable great room, an owners' club, and a year- round storage locker. There was an external-exchange affiliate as well as an opportunity to take short-notice weekend vacations.*

## **A** Use Right

1/4 interest or twelve weeks per year

## **B** Use System

Deeded interest (1/4 share to unit 678)

Purchase contract

Disclosure documents

Declaration

Estimated operating budget

CC&Rs

Management rules and regulations

Exchange affiliate agreement

Physical description

## **C** Use Management Plan

Owner use rules and regulations (including dues and fees)

Procedures for reservations including:

1) Fixed week with a rotating calendar
2) Space available program (Short-notice vacation reservation procedures)
3) Procedures for using the external exchange program (including additional fees)

Let's look at a hypothetical non-equity destination club offering.

*Martin Baker, an investment banker, and his wife, June, have the economic resources to vacation in some of the world's most coveted resorts. They have three college-aged children, as well as a large extended family and friendship network. They travel at least three to four weeks every year and typically stay in five-star hotels or resorts. They expect great service when they travel and are prepared to pay for it.*

*Martin and June are now discovering their three children are starting to have separate active lives. They still want to stay connected, and traditionally the family has always found time to vacation together. But the size of the hotel rooms in which Martin and June usually stay can't accommodate their children and the friends they want to bring along. They've read about non-equity destination clubs, seen pictures of the beautiful homes and villas from the promotional material, and spoke to a friend who had a membership. After doing their research, they decide to submit an application to join. They were accepted by the club and decided on a Gold Membership, which allowed them twenty-five days per year of use. There was a one-time refundable membership fee and annual dues.*

**A** **Use Right**

Twenty-five days per year

**B** **Use System**

Member application

Club membership agreement (includes all policies on use, membership, deposit, dues, financial reporting policies, resignation policies, termination policies)

**C** **Use Management Plan**

Membership rules and regulations including:

1) Procedures for paying annual dues
2) Procedures for transferring a membership
3) Procedures for financial accountability of the club to the member
4) Reservation procedures
5) Procedures for resignation

## Shared Ownership/Use Abridged: Choices

## TIMESHARE

A good choice for families who:

✓ Want to vacation in a resort setting at least once a year or once every two years.

✓ Like to return to their favorite spot every year, and occasionally exchange for a vacation within the network of exchange resorts.

✓ Want to lock in the price of accommodations in perpetuity.

✓ Like the amenities of full kitchens and accommodations larger than typical hotel rooms.

# FRACTIONALS AND PRIVATE RESIDENCE CLUBS

A good choice for families who:
- ✓ Consider owning a second home but don't like the idea of the cost and maintenance associated with it.
- ✓ Want to return year after year to their favorite location.
- ✓ Want larger, more luxurious accommodations than typical hotel rooms.
- ✓ Have the disposable income to make a large investment in a shared-ownership residence, and are able to meet the financial obligations of annual dues.
- ✓ Want more personalized service than those offered by resort hotels.
- ✓ Want a deeded interest.

# DESTINATION CLUBS

A good choice for families who:
- ✓ Want the opportunity to vacation with family and friends in very large, luxurious residences around the world.
- ✓ Want extraordinary service, and a 24/7 concierge.
- ✓ Want a luxury vacation in many different destinations in a single year.
- ✓ Are interested in unique experiential vacations with the travel and concierge service component.
- ✓ Want the privacy offered in these residences that is not common in hotels.

✓ Have the financial independence to participate at the top end of the leisure travel industry.
✓ Are not concerned about an equity position in the real estate portfolio, *and are comfortable with the non-equity club concept.*

Now that you have the tools, we can look into the details of the various offerings in the shared ownership/use industry, then understand how they can fit particular lifestyles, and where the best fit may be for your family.

> *"Thank you, Q, but this time I've got the gadgets and I know how to use them."*

James Bond - On Her Majesty's Secret Service, 1969

# 2

Chasing the Big Vacations One Week at a Time:
Traditional Timeshare Redux

*"It's never too late to have a happy childhood."*

Tom Robbins

## Introduction

When I was a kid growing up in the fifties (a little after Pearl Harbor but before Britney Spears), my mother would occasionally treat us to a box of Lucky Elephant Pink Popcorn (similar to Cracker Jack). Inside the box of delicious cotton candy–pink popcorn was a small prize – usually a plastic toy or a whistle. Stamped on the tag or the bag of the toy was the designation "Made in Japan." The "Made in Japan" label was prevalent in all small and cheap imported items like the small prizes in popcorn boxes, children's toys, and inexpensive household gadgets.

It is hard to imagine today, because the Japanese economy in the twenty-first century is manufacturing and exporting sophisticated electronic equipment and computers all around the world.

I share this story with you, because all too often when you talk about timeshare, some folks roll their eyes, groan and knowingly say, "Yes, I know about timeshare." Hey, folks, in the last twenty years, the timeshare industry has changed dramatically. Nine out of ten timeshare intervals are deeded. Most states have regulated the industry, and the industry has welcomed the regulations. The offerings, accommodations, exchange programs, member services, and added-value programs are simply astounding, with major brands dominant players in the industry.

Japanese products over the years became desirable consumer goods through quality, product development, and innovation. The same goes for timeshare. The vacation ownership industry of today is not your mama's timeshare.

## A Short History

It is generally acknowledged that in the 1960s, a ski resort in the French Alps offered the first timeshare with a catchy advertising slogan: "It's cheaper to buy the hotel than to rent the room." Laugh if you will, but this little slogan was what could be described as the proverbial snowball that started rolling down Mont Blanc. In 2008, timeshare sales were $9.7 billion and contributed $77 billion to the U.S. economy.[1]

In the U.S., Innisfree Corporation, located in Sausalito, California, put the original "deeded ownership" timeshare program forward in 1973. In a joint venture with a Hyatt franchisee, Innisfree's first development, headed by Carl Berry, was at Brockway Springs in Lake Tahoe, California, and became the first deeded ownership timeshare in the world.[2] For the subsequent fifteen years, the product known as "fixed-week" ownership was the industry standard.

But as air travel became more accessible, owners began to desire greater flexibility in where, how, and when they spent their vacations. In 1984 Marriott became the first branded hospitality company to enter the timeshare industry and remained so for nearly a decade.

Points were initially used by Vacation Internationale in the Pacific Northwest, and in 1991 Wyndham Vacation Ownership (at the time Fairfield Communities) became one of the major U.S. developers to move from traditional fixed-week timeshare ownership to a *points-based* exchange program with the launch of FairShare Plus. This forever changed the face of the timeshare industry with points-based programs providing far greater value and flexibility.

## They've Got You Covered

In 1977 only three U.S. states regulated timesharing. By the end of the 1980s, thirty-eight of the fifty states had passed specific timeshare laws, with lawmakers in the other twelve states amending existing laws to cover timeshare sales.[3]

Since the definition of timeshare as a "use right" is applicable to all shared vacation and/or leisure real estate accommodations, all shared real estate property with prepaid use plans, regardless of the length of the use right, is protected under individual state timeshare regulations.

The timeshare industry today benefits from a significant degree of organization and regulation. In the United States, ARDA (American Resort Development Association) advocates for high standards of ethical professional conduct in the industry, and also serves as an advocacy organization for the industry. Established in 1969, ARDA today has over a thousand members ranging from privately held firms to publicly traded companies and international corporations with expertise in shared-ownership interests in leisure real estate.

Today, there are 7 million intervals owned, and that does not include fractionals or private residence clubs.[4]

The ARDA Web site, accessible at www.arda.org, lists developer members. A new ARDA consumer Web site designed to educate the consumer about vacation ownership products, including tips on the buying and selling process, can be accessed at www.VacationBetter.org

## The New Vacation Industry: From Sedona to Safaris

"Vacation Ownership" is the new moniker for the traditional timeshare portion of the shared-ownership/use industry. The name is apt for several reasons. First, "vacation ownership" removes the notion that you are sharing in the purchase price of a "place" and that you are purchasing "vacation options," and provides a truer understanding. Second, it removes any idea that buying a timeshare implies a financial investment, which it is not. Third, the traditional one-week timeshare of the seventies bears little resemblance to the offerings, the regulations, or the reputation of the industry today.

The industry has been transformed from its early incarnation as an inflexible fixed-week product to a fluid, responsive, flexible marketplace offering a cornucopia of resort accommodations, exchange opportunities, cruise getaways, and experiential options from safaris to wine-tasting.

## National Brand Power

National brands, including Marriott, Hyatt, Wyndham, Starwood, and Hilton, have brought their brand power to the industry with stunning results. The sheer size of the resort holdings and membership numbers are staggering.

For example, Wyndham Vacation Ownership has become the world's largest vacation ownership company, with more than 830,000 owner families and more than 20,000 vacation ownership units in 150 resorts throughout North America, the Caribbean and the South Pacific. Marriott Vacation Club has more than 50 resorts and more than 400,000 owners. Hilton Grand Vacations has 33 affiliated resorts and 148,000 members, who through their Club membership, gain access to 3,300 hotels in the worldwide Hilton Family.

Starwood Hotels and Resorts includes such brand names as Westin, Sheraton, and St. Regis, with Starwood Vacation Club offering a program that gives members access to 850 hotels and resorts in more than 95 countries around the world.

There are smaller clubs too, which are just as impressive in what they offer. Hyatt Vacation Club entered the industry in 1994 with its first property, Hyatt Sunset Harbor in Key West, Florida. Hyatt's focus and the key to its success has been the considerable planning and research it does for every project. They have 15 resort locations, each with a distinct "boutique" quality to it. As with most major vacation ownership companies, Hyatt offers owners an internal exchange program. Hyatt Gold Passport® is a program that provides owners the opportunity to stay in over 730 Hyatt Hotels and resorts in 45 countries worldwide and is affiliated with a major vacation exchange company that extends travel opportunities to more than 2,200 resorts around the world.

Another prime example of the success of the "boutique" vacation ownership clubs is the story of Intrawest, the developer behind the great ski resort in Whistler, British Columbia. In 1994 Club Intrawest's members were mostly "West Coasters" enamored with the club's one location: Whistler. Asked what their membership was at the time, they said they could count the number of members on two hands. The private exchange program was just a vision. Club Intrawest today is an international private resort club with eight locations in exclusive ski, golf, and beach destinations in the U.S., Canada, and Mexico with more than 40,000 members from 47 countries. They have also developed an innovative internal exchange program called ExtraOrdinary Escapes.

## Vacation Ownership Brands

Vacation ownership brands continue to thrive and expand. In 1999, after two decades of selling vacation ownership, Shell Vacations, now one of the nation's largest independent vacation ownership development companies, introduced its points-based club, Shell Vacations Club (SVC). Today, with 23 locations and 125,000 members, the club offers not only access to vacation choices in accommodations around the world, but experiential vacations such as adventure travel, eco-tourism, and educational trips, as well as region-specific vacations like golfing in Arizona and skiing in Canada.

Bluegreen Resorts has over 40 resorts within its network spanning the continental U.S., Hawaii, and the Caribbean, offering a wide range of vacationing experiences to its over 185,000 members.

Diamond Resorts International continues to be among the leaders, with 109 resort locations throughout the United States, Hawaii, Mexico, Europe, the Caribbean, and Canada.

## Discovery Model Applied to Timeshare

When introduced to the plans, exchanges, types of owner-ship, fees, calendars, and reservation systems, there seems to be an overwhelming amount of information to digest. Most sales presentations last ninety minutes, and there's a lot of ground to cover. The salesperson usually picks up on what interests you most, for example the exchange opportunities, and they will spend an inordinate amount of time explaining how simple it is.

To investigate the different offerings that make vacation ownership such a compelling lifestyle investment for so many families, we can use the Discovery Model to differentiate what is being offered and present the innovations and opportunities that could lay a foundation for "owning" your vacations.

### **A** Use Right
> Let's recall use right. Timeshare is a prepaid use right for less than a year for multiple years in a vacation ac-commodation or leisure real estate property.
> In the traditional vacation ownership model, use right is typically one week.

### **B** Use System
The most common form of ownership or membership:

## Fee Simple or Deeded

➤ Like with home ownership, you own legal title to the share or the *use right* of the accommodation purchased. The deed is the legal document providing title to the property. Nine out of ten U.S. vacation ownership resorts provide a fee-simple deed with title insurance.[5]

➤ Each unit in a resort development is divided into fifty-two week-long shares (or fifty-one, if the resort "removes" one week for annual maintenance). The buyer purchases the use right share of the unit, either for a specific week or for a floating week within the season. For example, in the case of a fixed week, if a buyer were to purchase the share associated with *week 21* in unit *123,* they would receive a deed conveying to them ownership of that specific timeshare fraction. In floating-weeks or points systems, the deed may simply convey the ownership to a non-specific week as a means of securing access to the use system. For example, the deed might state that the owner owns an undivided $1/52^{nd}$ (or $1/51^{st}$) interest in unit 123.

➤ Since a timeshare deed is a real estate transaction, it will be recorded with a local government agency, such as a county recorder or assessor. Since ownership in a deeded property is ownership of real estate, the owner can sell the timeshare unit, give it away or bequeath it to his or her heirs, just as with other real property.

## Deed of Trust

➤ In the deed-of-trust mechanism, the ownership deed is held in trust by a bank, trust company or financial institution on behalf of the owner which grants a "right to use" through an owner's certificate. This mechanism can be used for some types of vacation ownership that use "points" or "credits" in their reservation system.

## Right-to-Use (RTU)

> ➤ In a right-to-use regime, the buyer has the right to use the unit for a specified number of years. At the end of that period, the usage rights return back to the property owner, who continuously owns the underlying title. The buyer can usually sell, donate or bequeath a right-to-use contract, but the expiration date will remain the same.
> ➤ Timeshare ownership in countries outside the U.S. and in most major metropolitan areas in the United States typically follows a right-to-use system.

## Leasehold

> ➤ Leasehold is a form of property tenure where one party buys the right to occupy a building for a fixed length of time (in the case of timeshare, purchasers buy the use right for a fixed period of time, often measured in decades). A leasehold interest does provide the same basic ownership rights and protections and may include a first right to renew the interest at the end of the fixed period of the contract.
> ➤ Vacation ownership leaseholds may occur in areas where regulations may prohibit ownership, such as Mexico, England, and some U.S. metropolitan areas.

## Club Membership (Trust Mechanism/Internal Exchange Mechanism)

> ➤ Much like a golf club membership, the member pays a certain amount to join the club for a certain amount of time, with annual dues. At the end of the stated term, the membership reverts back to the developer.
>
> ➤ Most vacation ownership companies that use "club" in their titles (for example, Marriott Vacation Club and Hyatt Vacation Club) use the term as a marketing term and are, in fact, a variety of exchange and reservation services, and vacation and travel benefits offered by the vacation ownership company to owners of deeded interests in resorts affiliated with the vacation ownership company, not "club memberships" per se.

# Sealing the Deal

Transactions are governed by individual states and legal requirements by individual developers will vary from state to state. Below is a list of documents that may apply to the transaction for timeshare and fractional interest projects.

## Purchase Contract

> ➤ The purchase contract is the legally binding document that defines the relationship between the seller and the buyer, including the terms of the sale, the rights and obligations of the parties, time lines for completion, and any actions necessary to close the sale. The purchase contract must be in writing. Make sure you understand all

the terms to which you are committing. There should be a rescission period (typically three to seven days) in the contract in keeping with individual state requirements.

## Disclosure Document

> Part of the real estate sales transaction, this form varies from state to state, but includes the description and condition of the project, plans for completion, and management information.

## Declaration of Timeshare Plan

> A document describing the timeshare use plan, including establishment of the homeowners association and proposed bylaws, amendment rules and at what point control will pass from the developer to the homeowners association. This document can also outline the policies and procedures that are the foundation of the "use management plan." The Declaration of Timeshare Plan may be incorporated into an underlying real estate regime document such as a Declaration of Condominium as CC&Rs.

## Estimated Operating Budget

> A document estimating the resort's operating costs, contributions to the reserve fund, any revenues as well as the amount of the annual maintenance fee (HOA dues) per unit week for units of various sizes.

## Covenants, Conditions and Restrictions (CC&Rs)

> ➤ This document outlines the written rules, limitations, and restrictions on the use of the property as well as stating what can and cannot be done with the property. It may also include, for example, limitation on pets, use of barbeques, and conduct. Restrictive covenants are intended to enhance property values by controlling development.

## Management Agreement and Rules and Regulations

> ➤ A document describing property use, property management, owners' use rights, the conduct of management, guest policies, and other operational issues. Depending on the structure, this document may outline the policies and procedures that are the foundation for the "use management plan."

## Physical Description

> ➤ A document describing the resort property; includes a survey, a plot plan, floor plans, and a written legal description.

### **C** Use Management Plan

The use management plan outlines the programs and services that are offered to the owner/member and how those programs and services can be used. It provides the action plan to the rules and regulations for paying annual fees and taxes.

The use methods outlined, describe the *type* of program offered, for example, points or fixed week. The reservation systems then determine the *process and rules* for making the vacation reservation. For example, more points will be "spent" on a week in high season than for the same unit at the same resort in low season.

The management plan is designed to match a particular family's lifestyle and vacation needs with the resort. If the resort utilizes a point system, for example, and a family needs a set vacation week during the year, it may not be the best fit. If, however, a family has the flexibility to vacation at any time of the year, and has a strategy to book early, the points program may be an excellent fit.

Now let's look at the options developers have to create the value proposition for their resorts. It is important to remember that, although the categories are defined, a particular management plan can incorporate portions of any category to create a unique plan.

## Use Methods

### *Fixed Week/Fixed Unit*

> The fixed week/fixed unit is a program whereby an owner has a use right for a specific unit during a specific week of the year. The resort will have an annual reservation calendar outlining "weeks," usually starting at the first of the year. For example, an owner may have the use right to unit 456 for week 26 (which normally includes the forth of July holiday). The owner of that week has the use right for that week, in that unit, every year.
>
> There is also the option of fixed week/floating unit, whereby the week is fixed and the size of the unit is fixed (e.g. two bedroom) but a specific unit is not guaranteed.

## *Floating or Flex Time*

➢ This is a week that could be used anytime during a designated season (summer, winter, low season, high season) at the resort based on availability. Depending on the resort reservation system, some floating weeks may be used throughout the year at the resort, while others may only be used during certain seasons. For example, a timeshare may be a floating winter week where competition for prime weeks such as Christmas, Presidents' Week, and spring break is high. The weeks when school is in session would not be in high demand. Some floating contracts exclude major holidays, which are sold as fixed weeks.

➢ The reservation system often includes the right to use a particular "size" of unit to accommodate the reservations as opposed to the use right of a specific unit. For example, the reservation request could be for a two-bedroom condo at the resort between May 1 and August 1.

➢ Both deeded and a "right-to-use" property can operate with either fixed or floating-week programs.

➢ Christmas, spring break, Thanksgiving, the Fourth of July weekend, Labor Day, Memorial Day, and Presidents' Week (in the ski resorts) are reserved quickly, so learning about the resort's reservation process and booking as early as the resort allows are essential.

➢ Some programs allow flexible usage seasonally or annually when space is available.

➢ If the week is to be used in an external exchange, the resort reservation typically must be made in advance of "depositing" with the exchange provider.

## Rotating

➢ Some timeshares have a program of rotating weeks. In an attempt to give all owners a chance to vacation during the holiday weeks, the weeks are rotated forward or backward through the calendar. One year the owner may have use of week 1, then week 2 the next year, and week 3 the year after that. The advantage of this method is that it gives each owner an equal opportunity for prime weeks and the security of knowing when they'll vacation, but it is not very flexible.

## Split Week

➢ Owners are able to split their week into smaller, three- or four-day time segments that can be used for multiple vacations throughout the year.

## Biannual

➢ Owners have use rights every other year.

## Points

➢ Points are a symbolic measurement of value. In a traditional timeshare points-based system, the timeshare week(s) deed is placed in a trust, and the use right is relinquished for "currency" called points or credits, to be cashed in for the location of the resort, the season, and the unit size desired. The developer assigns a specific number of points to establish a value for a particular unit size, unit type, season, and a variety of locations.

For example, larger units will "cost" more points than smaller units, and in ski areas (December, January, and February or "high season") will "cost" more points than "low season" (for example, in July or August).

➢ The number of points required to obtain accommodations will usually vary based on:

- The popularity of the resort location
- The size of accommodations
- The number of nights of occupancy
- The nights requested (weekends and holidays usually require more points)
- The season

➢ Every vacation ownership resort will have a unique points program in its use management plan. Some points programs sell different types of points, with the more valuable points having higher priority in reserving accommodations during peak-demand periods. Most programs allow the buyer to accumulate points from the past year or borrow points from the next year, so buyers may trade to a larger unit, more popular resort, or high season if they are willing to travel less often. Many points programs allow for weekend vacations, short-term vacations, and off-season vacations at reduced point rates, as well as redemption of points for services and such goods such as airline tickets and automobile rentals.

➢ Flexibility is generally the biggest benefit to a resort program offering the points system. For those who don't need a fixed week, this type of program offers latitude in unit types, sizes, seasons, and resorts based on the number of points owned or points "spent." So for families whose vacation needs vary (for instance, one year they may need a two-bedroom, the next year only a one-bedroom), this program works well.

## Reservation Methods

Each vacation ownership club will match its reservation process to compliment its use program. For example, in some reservation programs, even though you have a "fixed week," you may still have to book the reservation six months in advance. Points programs typically start every year with an allotted number of points and can be used within the year, with reservations allowed twelve months in advance. Some clubs allow you to "save" or "borrow" points. Short-term bookings are typical in most points programs, but the procedure and rules for reserving the days will be distinct to every club.

Every club will have a unique and nuanced reservation plan, and clubs provide colorful calendars and guides to make the reservation process as clear as possible. It still can be, however, a seemingly complicated process because, for example, high and low seasons vary across the country, point values may not be consistent from one resort to another, and reservation windows differ for the type of reservation you may want. However, the terminology used is fairly consistent and it should provide a good starting point.

Reservation terminology that you should be familiar with:

### Reservation Window
The amount of time allowed to make a reservation.

### Home Resort
The resort where you purchased your week.

### Reservation Calendar
An annual calendar outlining arrival and departure dates, high and low seasons, unit sizes, and is used for booking reservations.

### Use Year
A twelve-month period of time beginning on the date specified in the membership/ownership agreement.

### Resort Point Values
Designed to reflect the value of the week and unit size purchased in a particular resort. There is no industry standard for point values; each developer designs a unique plan. (One vacation ownership club can offer 10,000 points for a week and another can offer 50,000 points for the same week). However, within a resort, there is a consistency to the point values. For example, to reserve a large unit in a high season will "cost" more points than a large unit in low season. Calendars and guides are provided to the owner that summarize point values and how to redeem them for vacation time.

### Weekly Charts
Charts that identify particular weeks during the year that are special in some way. For example, holiday weeks or weekends, peak times, high, low, mid-seasons, and off-season. Many marketing departments have given names to these weeks, in an attempt to make them easier to remember. So you may find the off-season called "Relax Season," or December/January in a ski resort called "Holiday Season."

## Deposit a Week

This is part of the reservation process where an exchange is requested. In some cases, in order to make an exchange, the week must be made available (deposited) to the exchange company before a request for a destination can be processed.

## Banking Points/Borrowing Points

Many resorts that use the point system, allow banking of resort points for a period of a year so that an owner/member can save up points to take a vacation that uses more points than they have for one year, or if they cannot take a vacation in a particular year. There are also programs that allow "borrowing" all or potions of allotted resort points from the following year to use in the current year.

# Fees

## Annual Fees

> ➤ To maintain the quality and future value of the resort property and property management services, owners are charged an annual "maintenance fee" or "homeowners fee." The fees, which are set up and directed by the HOA (Home Owners Association) or club, pay for on-site management, unit upkeep and refurbishment, utilities, insurance, and maintenance of the resorts' amenities and common areas. They are essential in ensuring that the resort where you stay is well maintained and updated.

> ➤ Depending on the resort's location and the policy in the rules and regulations, the annual fee may or may not include the real estate property tax.
> ➤ A portion of the maintenance fee should be set aside in a reserve fund to pay for major repairs and improvements. The resort documents should estimate the maintenance fee, include the reserve fund and reserve fund allocation.
> ➤ If the cost for an improvement or repair that was unforeseen by the board of directors (if it was caused, for example, by a natural disaster or an accident) is not in the budget, a single charge to cover the expense called a "special assessment," can be levied against the owner or owners.

## Property Tax

> ➤ A property tax is levied against timeshare resorts, because they are real estate. In many cases, the resort sends an annual bill that includes both your portion of the property tax (based on your ownership interest) and maintenance (HOA) fees.

## Housekeeping Fees

> ➤ Resorts may charge a daily/weekly housekeeping fee to have rooms cleaned, beds made-up, and garbage removed.

## Exchange and Membership Fees

> ➤ Many resorts will throw in one year of membership dues to join the external exchange affiliate. After that, it is typically the owner's decision to continue with an annual fee. Domestic and international exchange

fees apply when making an exchange through these companies, as does, in some cases, a daily housekeeping fee.

➤ Some resorts charge a fee to become a member of internal programs such as points or usage based bonus programs within a hotel group.

➤ Housekeeping fees are typically charged to the visitor/owner, so in either an internal or external exchange, the fee will be applied.

### *Additional Taxes*

➤ Bed tax, occupancy tax, or transient tax may be applicable in some jurisdictions.

### *Recreation/Activity/Service Fees*

➤ For such services as housekeeping, exchanges, memberships to programs rentals of recreational equipment, and activities like horseback riding, golf, or skiing, additional fees could apply. Discounts on rates may or may not apply.

## Value-Added Programs

In addition to the internal and external exchange opportunities, many vacation ownership companies have ways of enhancing their club and adding value for their members. The development of these value-added programs, which can include Broadway tickets, trial memberships, travel bookings, airline tickets, and meals in Paris are making vacation ownership even more attractive.

Many of the brands, for example Wyndham, Hilton, Starwood, Hyatt, and Marriott, include exchanges and benefits that include the hotel chains and reward programs affiliated with the parent company. Remember, some of these programs may have additional fees, so you should weigh the use/cost benefit.

## Vacation Exchange Programs

One of the great benefits of owning timeshare is the ability to "trade" or "exchange" a week (or points/credits) in your home location for another owner's week at a different resort. The exchange program provides the opportunity to travel and experience exciting locations throughout the world.

One year you may want to ski the Rockies. The next year bask in the Florida sunshine, or perhaps try authentic Italian food – in Florence! Dying to be insulted in France when you try out your high school French? A quick "au revoir" and you should be on your way. There are so many options with so many places to explore that it will be hard to choose. Many families have had splendid debates over where their next vacation should be!

Exchange vacations are a great solution when you want to change the annual weeks (or points) you've been assigned at your resort. If you understand how exchanges work, plan ahead, sprinkle a little flexibility into the mix, you should be sipping that café Americano in no time.

As with all things in timeshare, there is more than one exchange system. There is the *internal exchange* within your resort family, and there is the "affiliate partner exchange company" (also called *external exchange*), a company employed by timeshare owners to provide a larger range of options.

## How The Exchange System Works

Both internal and external exchanges are based on availability. Essentially, space becomes available by members depositing their timeshare week into an exchange inventory "bank." After a member deposits their week, a request for an exchange *can* be made. If the request can be matched with existing space bank inventory, the exchange *is* made. If the accommodation requested is not available because no one has deposited that particular week at that resort with the unit size requested, the member can change the request to a different resort (or a different time or unit size), or they can initiate a search to track future availability. Consider two or three choices for your exchange vacation; flexibility is the key to making successful exchanges.

## Internal Exchange

Most large vacation clubs will have an internal exchange program, that is, an exchange opportunity between properties in the same family of resorts. When you purchase a timeshare week, the resort that you signed your contract with is called the "home" resort. There is always a "home resort advantage" for members, giving them every opportunity to return and enjoy their resort.

Most plans give members ample opportunity and planning time to book a week at their home resort, and reduced planning time to book exchanges. (Remember, an exchange can happen only if there is an available unit and that occurs if someone deposits their home resort unit in the inventory bank). But when they do want to visit another resort in the "family," they have the best chance of making the exchange if they book early.

Some clubs operate on a points-based system where there is no "home resort" advantage. Members simply book on a first-come, first-served basis and book their stay based on point value and availability. Every club will have a unique reservation system to facilitate these exchange requests, as well as a unique fee structure for usage, exchange, housekeeping, and so on.

As you can see, the use management plan pillar in the Discovery Model is elaborate, because it deals with the "nuts and bolts" of how programs are defined, and how families can use their use right. Every development will have a unique management plan, and that is why it is important to match what a particular plan offers to the needs of the your family. Of course, some of you might be lucky enough to have all your priorities met with a particular resort; price, use system, location, use right, reservation system, exchange opportunities and managed rentals, but more likely, you will have to prioritize the items that are an absolute deal breaker. Once you have determined what the essential "must-haves" are in a vacation ownership opportunity for your family, weigh the overall management plan accordingly.

Let's look at two real-life examples that include some of the concepts we've talked about. Hyatt Vacation Club not only incorporates both a fixed week concept and a points program that allow the owner a fixed week when needed, but also the flexibility of converting the week to points; Club Intrawest uses a points-based system with a first-come, first-served reservation plan.

Here is a short excerpt from HYATT VACATION CLUB member news: Please note that these excerpts are used for illustration purposes only and are partial examples that may be dated and/or changed. Hyatt Vacation Club always provides complete and current owner's manuals to owners.[6]

---

### How to Make Reservations and Use Your Points

Many members find that reserving their unit and week of purchase becomes a tradition. So each year they call during their **Home Resort Preference Period** to let us know they will be returning to their home resort on their week of purchase. Remember, while the Home Resort Preference Period window lets us hold your fixed week exclusively for you, Hyatt Vacation Club does not make the reservation for you. Your Home Resort Preference Period also expires six months prior to your fixed week.

To make any other type of reservation, you will convert your fixed week to points. In doing so, here are a few things to consider:

### When do you want to travel?

Consult the reservation calendars, which reflect the dates for Friday, Saturday, and Sunday arrivals. Be sure to confirm the day and date of arrival for your selected week, because each year the calendar varies by a few days.

---

### How many points are in your account?

As you pass through each reservation window, a statement is mailed explaining the reservation window and number of points in your account. To determine point values, locate the destination choice on the "Season Week" chart, look to the week you intend to travel, then go to the "Point Values" chart for the unit size. This will tell you how many points are needed for a reservation. If you travel in off seasons, you can often make two or more reservations from one allotment of points.

### Options outside Hyatt Vacation Club

Beyond Hyatt Vacation Club resorts, Interval International is an option during your Home Resort Preference Period or your Club Use Period. This allows you to use all or any portion of points toward exchanges at any Interval International resorts worldwide. Every day Interval members exchange travel weeks, which means availabilities change daily. Unsure of your travel plans and considering destinations outside your Hyatt Vacation Club? You have the option of using the Extended External Exchange Program. Members may commit all or any portion of their fixed week or float points to the Extended External Exchange Program for the purposes of exchange through Interval International for two years.

> Fixed points must be converted into the program four months before their deeded week commences. Once points are transferred to the Extended External Exchange Program, they cannot be returned to a Hyatt Vacation Club account.

In the Hyatt example, where there is a home resort and owners have purchased a specific week, the guide provides details and reminders about how and when to book as well as details on exchanging a fixed week to points.

Let's look at a club example. Since Club Intrawest's management plan includes "points" (and not a week that has an option to converts to points), there is no "home resort." Reservations are on a first-come, first-served basis. Here are several excerpts from the club membership owner's manual. Please note that these excerpts are used for illustration purposes only and are partial examples that may be dated and or changed. Club Intrawest always provides complete and current owner's manuals to members[7].

> **Resort Points**
>
> Your membership with Club Intrawest gives you an annual allotment of Resort Points. You use these Resort Points to reserve accommodation at Club Intrawest locations or travel to ExtraOrdinary Escapes destinations.

## Your Use Year

You have 12 months to travel using your annual allotment of Resort Points. This period is referred to as your "Use Year" and it begins on the date specified on your Membership and Resort Points Certificate. Your Resort Points are allocated annually at the start of each Use Year. Use Years are established at the time of purchase and follow the lifetime of a Membership. They cannot be changed. Make your vacation request as early as possible so we can help you create the vacation you want. When making reservations, your Resort Points are withdrawn from the Use Year in which your travel dates occur. You do not need to wait until the beginning of your Use Year to make reservations.

**You will want to plan in advance how to use your Resort Points each Use Year, as they expire if not used or banked.**

## When do members make their vacation plans?

Use the following guide for when Members generally make their vacation plans:

| | |
|---|---|
| Holiday Season | 11 months in advance |
| Peak Season | 6 to 11 months in advance |
| Activity Season | 1 to 6 months in advance |
| Opportunity Season | 1 to 3 months in advance |
| Relax Season | 1 to 3 months in advance |

**Your ExtraOrdinary Escapes Membership**

Membership in ExraOrdinary Escapes is optional for Club Intrawest Members. In order to enjoy vacations through ExtraOrdinary Escapes, you pay an annual Membership Fee. Check with Member Services for the current Membership Fee.

**Making Your Reservation Requests**

You can begin planning your ExtraOrdinary Escapes vacation up to a maximum of 12 months prior to your travel date. Refer to the Web site at www.clubintrawest. com for reservation details including Resort Point values for each of the destinations.

Note: ExtraOrdinary Escapes is the exchange network that has been created by Club Intrawest for use by its members.

The partners include:

**Hilton Grand Vacation Club**

Members have direct access to 8 Hilton Grand vacation Clubs in Hawaii, Orlando, Miami and Las Vegas.

Hilton H Honors – As part of the relationship with Hilton Grand Vacation Club, members of ExtraOrdinary Escapes are automatically eligible for Hilton HHonors.

Silver VIP Membership – Members may convert their Club Intrawest Resort Points to Hilton HHonors Points to make reservations at over 2500 hotels in the 8 Hilton Family Brands of Hotels and reserve cars with 2 major car rental companies.

**Disney Vacation Clubs**

Experience the magic of Disney with their vacation ownership product. With your ExtraOrdinary Escapes Membership, you have direct access to all 7 Disney Vacation Club locations. Five of them are located within Walt Disney World in lake Buena Vista, Florida, one is in Vero Beach, Florida, and one is located on Hilton Head in South Carolina.

**Resort Condominiums International (RCI)**

RCI is the world's leading timeshare exchange provider with over 3 million members worldwide and 4,000 affiliate resorts in 101 countries.

**Resort to Resort Destinations**

Resort to Resort is the exclusive Intrawest homeowner exchange program. Through Resort to Resort, Members of ExtraOrdinary Escapes have access to Intrawest destination resorts. There are also a number of carefully selected resort locations outside of the Intrawest network, including Costa Rica and Florida.

**Hotels & Resorts**

This is ExtraOrdinary Escapes' unique collection of hand selected resorts and hotels from around the world. Some are one-of-a-kind gems, while others belong to such prestigious associations as Relais et Chateaux or Small Luxury Hotels of the World. Also represented in the collection are major luxury hotel operators like Fairmont and Four Seasons.

**Cruising Adventures (ICE)**

ExtraOrdinary Escapes provides a cruise program in partnership with many of the world's leading cruise companies, including Carnival, Celebrity and Norwegian. There are 2000 itineraries to choose from for your cruise vacation.

Use the power of your ExtraOrdinary Escapes Membership to explore a converted villa among the vineyards of Tuscany or a French farmhouse at the foothills of the Alps in Provence. For the more adventurous, try a signature once-in-a-lifetime vacation with adventure partners like Abercrombie & Kent, Canadian Mountain Holidays and Rocky Mountaineer vacations. Whether it's a safari in Tanzania, hiking in the Rockies, or kayaking in the Pacific, you won't soon forget your Excursion adventure.

**Banking Resort Points**

Some years you may want to enjoy a vacation requiring more Resort Points than your annual allotment. To do this, you may bank any portion of your annual allotment of Resort Points from one Use Year to the following Use Year.

**Borrowing Resort Points**

You may borrow up to 100% of your Resort Points from your next Use Year to make a reservation in your current Use Year.

In the Club Intrawest example, since there is no "home resort" all members have an opportunity, based on reservation procedures, to book a reservation based on the number of points they have rather than on the use right at a specific property at a specific time.

*Affiliate Partner Exchange (External Exchanges)*

Companies that handle the external exchange have an elaborate system of collecting accommodation inventory from timeshare owners around the world and redistributing it. The exchange companies use an individual rating system to determine "value" for the weeks of every resort in the network. Size of unit, time of year, resort location, resort quality, and consumer ratings are some of the factors that determine the "value" of a particular week in particular resort.

Individual owners make the "deposits" and "withdrawals" within this system, and the exchange companies try to meet supply and demand.

Exchange companies charge an annual fee for membership, plus fees for domestic and international exchanges, as well as additional fees. The exchange companies often operate their own travel agencies, offering their members flights, car rentals, cruises, travel insurance, etc., at competitive prices. Additional fees may apply for these services.

To create a convenient way to facilitate an exchange, the resort will have a contractual relationship with a particular affiliate exchange company. When you purchase a timeshare, you will be offered membership in that exchange company. Most developers offer to pay the first-year membership, and after that, you will be required to pay an annual fee to remain a member. You are entitled, however, to join an independent exchange company which provides an exchange service.

The two largest exchange companies are:
1) Resort Condominiums International® (RCI)
2) Interval International® (II)

There are several smaller independent exchange companies that offer an exchange service to timeshare owners. They include:
➤ RedWeek.com
➤ San Francisco Exchange Company (SFX)
➤ Trading Places Exchange and Management Company
➤ Dial an Exchange
➤ Platinum Interchange
➤ Timex Direct Exchange System

Let's take a closer look at the two major players.

## Resort Condominiums International (RCI)

Founded in 1974 as an exchange service for condominium owners, RCI quickly became a driving force for growth within the timeshare industry and has been at the forefront of the vacation ownership industry ever since.

Subscribing members belong to one of the world's largest vacation-exchange communities, which entitles three million plus members participating in the exchange system with more than 4,000 affiliated resorts around the world. The membership program is called RCI® Weeks, and members access vacation services and benefits such as cruise vacations, a full-service travel agency, discounts on airfare, rental cars, hotel stays, and vacation packages. There is an annual membership fee and transaction fees associated with membership.

In 2000 RCI helped change the industry again by introducing the RCI Points® program, the world's first global points-based exchange system. RCI Weeks members can covert their "weeks" ownership into RCI Points and use those points like currency to customize length of stay, unit size and type, and saving or borrowing points to create their dream vacation. Car rentals, cruises, airline tickets and hotel stays are made available through the RCI Points Partner Program.

Vacation owners must be an RCI Weeks member to join RCI Points, and must convert their existing ownership. There is a fee for this conversion and transaction fees associated with RCI Points. RCI membership is limited to RCI affiliated resorts. RCI is part of Group RCI within the Wyndham Worldwide family of companies.
www.RCI.com

# Interval International (II)

Since its inception in 1976, Interval International has brought together approximately 2,500 resorts in more than 75 countries around the world in its vacation exchange network, with approximately 2 million members worldwide. There is a membership fee and additional exchange fees when using the II exchange program, and membership is limited to II affiliated resorts.

Interval International has teamed with travel and leisure industry leaders to create affinity programs for the Interval Gold®, a membership upgrade available for an additional fee, that includes discounts on Getaways, complimentary Hertz #1 Club Gold® membership, EPI Entertainment®, Gold Concierge® personal assistance and Interval Options®, which allows members to put resort time toward the purchase of a cruise, golf package, or a spa vacation.

Dedicated Member-Services Centers are maintained around the world to provide personal assistance, and members can make exchanges and related travel arrangements online and in real time. In addition to exchange, Interval offers year-round leisure benefits and services that enhance the value of vacation ownership.

www.IntervalWorld.com

### *Ancillary Travel Sellers*

# ICE (International Cruise & Excursions)

In 1997, Marcia and John Rowley introduced a cruise program that offered timeshare owners the opportunity to exchange their resort weeks (or points) toward cruises and experiential vacations. Affiliated with every major cruise line, ICE offers worldwide travel options including cruise, resort, hotel, and a complete collection of experiential tour vacations (including white water rafting, wine tasting tours through Italy, African safaris, ski holidays, escorted and group travel). Membership is limited to owners at affiliated resorts. ICE members do not pay an exchange fee. www.iceenterprise.com

When planning your vacation exchange, consider:

- <u>The location you want to explore</u> – determine if it's an area (e.g. Florida) or a location (e.g. Napa Valley) or perhaps a different country.
- <u>The time of year you want to travel</u> – this will determine how many points you may need or the value of your week.
- <u>Who will travel with you</u> (e.g. children or aging parents) – this will help you determine the size of accommodation and the type of experience you want.

---

*EXCHANGE TIPS*

✓ CONSIDER THE EXPERIENCE. Most importantly, decide what you're looking for when exchanging. Think about the "what" before you think about the "where." Not all places, unit sizes or destinations

---

are available at all times. Think about the activities and experiences your family would enjoy during your vacation. For example, if skiing is the activity your family wants to experience one winter, and you want to exchange your week in Florida for a winter ski resort week, try not to fixate on a particular place, e.g., the Canyons in Park City, but go for the experience. If your family needs some beach and relaxation time, focus on that experience rather than wanting to go a specific resort in Mexico.

✓ **BE FLEXIBLE AND ADAPTABLE.** Try not to set your heart on one location in one type of accommodation during a certain week. If vacation experience is the key, then you should be able to have a time frame (month/season), and a choice of locations and accommodations that could easily fit the experience.

✓ **PLAN IN ADVANCE.** Get in the habit of booking your vacation as early as possible.

✓ **Use MEMBER SERVICES.** One of the advantages of vacation ownership is that you are never alone. Club service members are there to help you plan your vacation all along the way. They can help with bookings, suggestions for great getaways, travel tips, and recommendations.

✓ **ENHANCE YOUR EXCHANGE POSSIBILITIES.** Use your points to your advantage. Know how far they will go if you exchange a larger unit for a smaller one and a high-season week in one place for several low-season weeks in another.

✓ **REMEMBER THE FEES.** There may be an additional fee for the exchange, nightly fees, and/or house-keeping fees, so make sure you know what additional charges you are responsible for.

## Vacation Ownership Buyer Motivations

➤ Want to "commit" to a lifetime of vacations and vacation possibilities.

➤ Prefer to stay in resort accommodations and locations.

➤ Want to have condominium or villa-style accommodations with full kitchens.

➤ Like to have the same type of accommodations each time you visit, as opposed to booking a random hotel room.

➤ Aspire to travel to a variety of locations around the world (through use of the exchange), and stay in resort accommodations.

➤ Eager to "lock" in the accommodation portion of the cost of your vacations.

➤ Like the flexibility in choosing experiential vacations, e.g., cruising, safaris, dude ranch vacations, etc.

➤ Want to create legacy vacation experiences for your family.

➤ Have an affinity for a particular resort or location and want to return every year.

## Questions to Ask Yourself About the Right Fit

✓ Do you want a fixed week/floating week or a points system?
That is, do you want to be guaranteed a particular week in a particular season, or any week in a particular season, or are you flexible enough for a points system?

✓ Does the accommodation and the resort fit your family? In other words, do the unit size and amenities of the resort fit what you want in a vacation – is there a pool for your children, access to a spa, activities that interest your family, and/or a location that you want to return to year after year?

✓ Does the management system of the resort offer you the alternative vacations you might want to enjoy in the future?
Are the exchange systems a good fit for your family? If you want experiential vacation options (cruising, rafting the Colorado River, wine tasting) does the management plan offer an exchange option that fits that desire for the future?

✓ Is a "brand" hotel/resort developer important to you? Why?

✓ Do you want to be able to drive to your resort every year, or can you fly to your destination every year?

✓ Is renting or selling your vacation ownership really important to you? This is an important question, because re-sales of timeshares can be difficult and frustrating.

Timeshare is not an investment, so don't consider vacation ownership if that your focus.

✓ Can you afford the commitment of association dues and property taxes every year? Typically, the annual dues are billed once a year and must be paid in full at that time.

✓ If you vacation with a pet, is the resort "pet friendly?" Does the resort have pet- friendly units? How many and what is their availability?

The following questions are helpful for anyone interested in vacation ownership but are by no means the only questions to ask. Every family has unique circumstances that should guide them. Remember, good questions get good answers.

Salespeople are there to answer your questions in full, and you should be prepared to ask as many as you like. Never feel pressured to purchase anything. Although a sales presentation typically lasts ninety minutes, you should feel comfortable asking all the questions you want, and feel free to leave after the presentation without making a purchase commitment.

## Tina and the Timeshare Tour

Let me tell you one more story. True story, but the name has been changed, mostly to protect me.

I have a friend named Tina. Great woman. She attended a timeshare sales presentation. Tina was very impressed with the salesman and excited to report that there was absolutely no pressure to buy anything.

She was also very excited about the company's exchange, telling me that she could go anywhere in the world. Because of the volume of information she was given, she was not aware that the exchange was with an external exchange affiliate, that there would be additional fees, and that there was a reservation process that might restrict where she wanted to go and when she wanted to travel. She wasn't sure if there was an internal exchange because she assumed "exchange" meant "exchange." She was told her maintenance fees were going to be $375 per year and that there would be an additional charge of $125 per week if she stayed for a week, but she couldn't remember why. She remembered that with points, she could stay *anywhere* in *any* hotel, even along the highways when she traveled by car.

What she did have written down on a white sheet of paper was 20,000 points, a cost of $11,000, a breakdown of developer financing that led to a circled figure of $225 per month, with an initial down payment of $1,100 and a promise of $1,000 off the price if she referred three friends. She had also written down and circled the number forty-five, and recalled the number meant that she would get wherever she wanted to go in the world if she could "short-book" the reservation, because she told the salesman she would be unable to plan a year in advance.

To be clear, the salesman probably said twenty things, and Tina heard perhaps three. Because she knew very little about timeshare and all the information was new to her, she was a little overwhelmed and retained only a portion of the things that sounded exciting.

Now, Tina may buy the timeshare or not. She has another appointment to go back and discuss the things that really matter to her lifestyle. She will ask if the company has an internal exchange – so that she can reserve time within the family of resorts (if there are any). She can get clarification on what her points "buy" – that is, whether they have a program that would allow her to stay in *any* hotel on *any* highway in the United States. She will ask about rental opportunities and about banking her points, in case she can't travel one year. She will ask who manages the club and what their history is. Since the club is brand new, she will ask what the percentage cap is on HOA dues per year. She will ask if the management plan includes short stays or space available. She will ask what the procedure is for guests. She likes to travel with her dog, so she will ask if the resort is pet friendly. She will ask in detail, about the external exchange program, booking and reservation procedures, and additional fees. She will get clarification on all additional fees, including the weekly use fee of $125.

Tina may be disappointed or more pleased than ever when she gets the answers that will help her decide if: a) timeshare is a good fit for her lifestyle, and b) this particular timeshare resort and company is a good fit.

What I do know is that if Tina decides to buy (with that $1,000 discount for referrals), I will be getting a call.

## General Questions
## Within the use system:

- ➢ What is the form of ownership? For example, deed, right-to-use, or club membership?
- ➢ What is the right of rescission period in the contract?
- ➢ What is the percentage of increase allowed for home-owners fees?

> ➢ Are there unaccompanied-guest privileges?
> ➢ What are the policies for special assessment?
> ➢ Have you been provided all legal documentation required by the state you are purchasing in?

# Within the management plan:

> ➢ How is the use right managed? By fixed week? By points?
> ➢ What is the reservation process?
> ➢ What is the value of my week/points in an external exchange?
> ➢ Is there an internal exchange, and if so, what hotels are in the program and what is the reservation process?
> ➢ What are the additional fees, including any exchange fees, maintenance fees, property tax, housekeeping fees, service fees, activity fees, program participation fees, and closing costs?
> ➢ What kind of owner support is in place?  Can I speak to a customer service rep to resolve any problems I may have after I purchase?
> ➢ Can reservations be made on the resort Web site?
> ➢ What programs are in place to keep owners informed on current events, changes, and updates?
> ➢ If financing through the developer, what costs are involved, what are the terms, and what is the rate of interest?
> ➢ Is the resort a member of ARDA?
> ➢ 1f you want to sell your timeshare, are there any services, amenities, or programs that do not transfer with your interest?
> ➢ Who is the resort's external exchange affiliate?

> ➢ What are the additional fees, including housekeeping, exchange, space-available or value-added programs?
> ➢ Are the property taxes included with the HOA fees?
> ➢ Are rentals permitted, and does the property management team have a rental program? What is the rental revenue split?

# 3

## Explore Beyond the Shore and Beyond the Share: *Fractionals and Private Residence Clubs*

> *"There is no cure for birth and death,*
> *save to enjoy the interval."*

George Santayana

## Introduction

Although the concept of traditional timeshare may be well known, one of the most exciting and recent innovations in the sale of resort real estate is the birth of fractional ownership. Many families wanted to have a second home in the resort area they loved, but the costs associated with buying and maintaining a whole ownership property was prohibitive, particularly when they only vacationed there a few times a year. Timesharing was not a good option for these folks, because they wanted to vacation more than one week a year, they really wanted a second home option, and they wanted more exclusivity to their resort than timeshare resorts were offering.

Whereas timeshares are sold on a week-by-week basis, fractional properties are sold with more use rights – typically three to twelve weeks, although a 1/24 share is now being offered in very exclusive "rare-air" locations. But the amount of use rights is only the tip of the iceberg. Prime locations, in addition to upscale ski destinations, now include beach, golf, and urban locations. Amazing amenities, spaciousness, finishes of the residences, services and, of course, the price are all part of the differentiators. Developers are offering five-star residences that boast state-of-the art kitchens, master suites, designer interiors, spa facilities, and concierge services. They offer the buyer the feeling of being in their own, extraordinarily furnished vacation home, with amazing amenities, at a fraction of the cost of owning and maintaining a luxury second home.

Service also plays a key role. You could arrive several times a year to your vacation home, have a valet park the car, experience preferential treatment at check-in, with the concierge welcoming you by name and tending to your every need. In some clubs, staff place family photos throughout the residence and stock the refrigerator with your favorite food and wine before your arrival, all to reinforce the notion that you are home.

Owner's clubs were created to offer a dimension of exclusivity to an already heady experience; exclusivity, prestige, and membership privilege are all words that are used to describe fractional ownership today.

## The Evolution of Fractional Ownership

In 1972, Carl Berry, one of the first developers to build and market timeshare properties, became an innovator again, in what is generally considered to be one of the first fractional properties, Sun River in Oregon. Sun River was a large homestead project which had 4,000 home sites and 1,000 condos, offered in 1/5 shares. And although the project was successful, Mr. Berry was ahead of his time and the fractional concept lay dormant for many years.

In 1990 the fractional property was reborn in spectacular form. Two businessmen, Steve Dering and Jim Whitteron launched the Deer Valley Club in Park City, Utah, with an offering of a 1/6 share. The Deer Valley Club offered luxurious condominiums at a competitive second-home price in a very prestigious and expensive ski resort.

Steve Dering is the founder of the luxury residence club concept and developed the prototype for today's high-end fractional industry. The private residence club has now become the generic term for the luxurious, upscale, prestigious sector of fractional resort properties. The success of the Deer Valley Club gave momentum to the fractional industry, particularly in posh ski resort areas in Colorado, where within seven years there were 24 fractionals and private residence clubs in one stage of development or another. In 2003 sales for the fractional industry reached $500 million.[1] In 2007, according to Ragatz Associates, the leading research firm in fractional ownership, sales exceeded $2.3 billion, with 300 fractional interval and private residence clubs (up from 254 in 2006) in North America, 153 of which were in active sales.[2]

Not surprisingly, acclaimed five-star hospitality brands such as Ritz-Carlton, St. Regis, Fairmont, and Grand Residences by Marriott, have climbed on board. Intrawest developed its fractional division, called "Storied Places" and have developed "Resort to Resort" a fractional-only exchange company.

Resort developers have managed and continue to secure the very best locations in the most beautiful and exciting places in the world, where they continue to build magnificent residences with amenities to match and are adding corporate partners to their roster to distinguish themselves in the marketplace. Urban residence clubs have added a new dimension to an industry that was, until a few years ago, primarily in resort real estate.

## What Is Fractional Real Estate?

There are currently two types of fractional interest real estate products – fractionals and private residence clubs. Both fractionals and PRCs are identified by deeded ownership of a use right interest in a high-value, luxury real estate accommodation, with a high standard of furnishings, finishes, amenities, hotel-type services, and the associated cost of HOA fees and property tax. The market for this type of real estate is affluent, well-traveled people who expect the best.

I was at a seminar for the fractional industry a few years ago, and a question was asked of the panel, "What is the difference between a fractional and a private residence club?" One gentleman on the panel stood up and said, "There is no difference between fractionals and private residence clubs, except price, location, amenities and service."

I laughed with rest of the attendees, because even those four items are pretty substantial, but what he was missing in his answer was how families intended to use the vacation home, and why they would choose to buy one over the other. Even though there are many similarities in the products, there are many differences that could influence a purchasing decision.

When I was working for American Skiing Company a few years ago as a management consultant, senior management sent me to Steamboat Springs, Colorado to help with the marketing efforts for their luxury fractional development, The Steamboat Grand. The town itself is very quaint and definitely western by design, but it's the great powder snow, Mt. Werner and the gorgeous Yampa Valley that's the real attraction. I have skied many places in North America and Europe with each resort area having its own appeal, but I will say, I have never skied on such great powder snow as I did on Mt. Werner.

There were a few other fractional developments being constructed while I was there, but our main "competition" was a private residence club called The Christie Club, which had a higher price point than we did. The sales manager and I walked over to Ski Time Square (I know, a bit corny – but these ski towns never miss an opportunity) to check out The Christy Club. It is a beautifully designed, well-built development with a warm, elegant ambiance and a ski-in ski-out location at the base of Mt. Werner. The club had amenities like an outdoor heated pool, jetted spas, a member lounge and so on, as well as an extensive service component. The Steamboat Grand had a pool and spa, as well as full conference facilities, 24/7 concierge and front desk, plus two great restaurants.

So what would make a family choose The Christie Club over The Steamboat Grand or vice versa? It's all in the details. For example, The Steamboat Grand offered a quarter-share (twelve weeks a year) in a specified unit with a rotating calendar. The Christie Club was a member owned club, where for a certain period of time, owners can make reservations and the balance of the year is open to space available bookings for all the owners, based on their reservation system. The Steamboat Grand offered a managed rental program, and the Christie Club did not. The Christie Club had a ski-in ski-out location. The Steamboat Grand was across the street from the ski resort. The Steamboat Grand was a seven-story, 164 unit development with underground parking. The Christie Club was smaller and more intimate with club automobiles for owner use.

There are more differences, but even with the ones I have mentioned, it is easy to see, that the two products have a different appeal. For some families, it is more important to have revenue potential with the managed rental program, than to be in a ski-in ski-out location. There are some families who want to stay in the same residence year after year, because it feels more like a second home, while some families want the flexibility of an open reservation system and it does not matter that the residence they stay in may be different with every visit. Some like the excitement of a large, bustling resort; others want the prestige of a member-only club. Some families want a ski-in ski-out location and will not consider anything else.

So, as I sat back in the Grand Ballroom in The Steamboat Grand that evening, I enjoyed a live concert by Lyle Lovett, surrounded by owners and guests who had decided that this was the place for them. And I must say, that same evening, owners of The Christie Club sat around the fireplace in their member's lounge, enjoying a hot cider with the same sentiments.

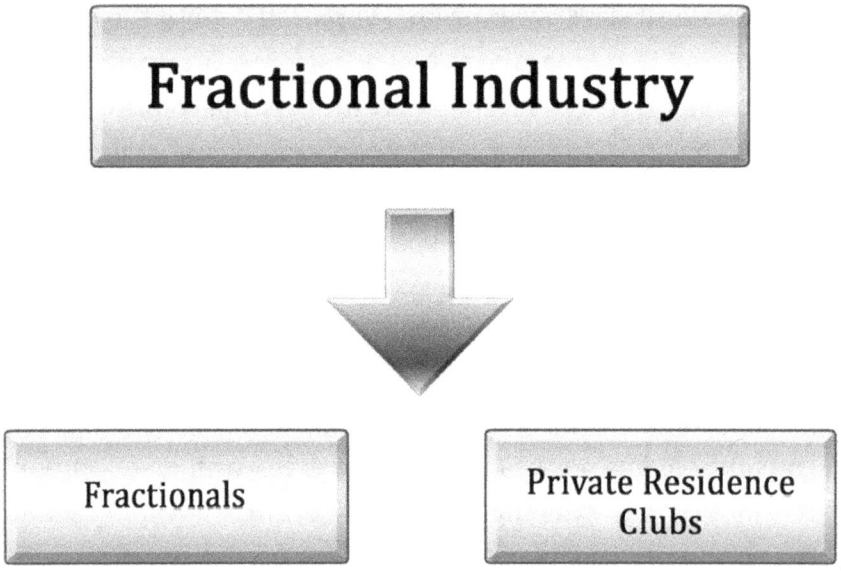

Fractional interest is defined as *a prepaid use right for less than one year, occurring for multiple years in one or more vacation or leisure accommodations.* It has the same definition as the one for timeshare. Why is this important? Because the same state legislation and legal frameworks designed to protect and safeguard timesharing consumers, also applies to fractionals and private residence club owners.

But how do fractional interests compare to timeshare?

- **Use Right** – The use right is more than one week and is typically two to twelve weeks. The use right is referred to as "shares," i.e., the ratio of owners per unit, as opposed to a timeshare "week."
- **Buyer Motivation** – Families who prefer fractional ownership typically return to the same place several times per year. For example, families have a favorite place to ski and they vacation there multiple times every winter. They have easy access (either by car or plane) and they use the residence as they would a second home. Timeshare owners typically buy a "vacation experience."
- **Size of Development** – Fractional developments are typically built on a smaller scale than timeshare developments, with membership more exclusive and private.
- **Configuration** – Fractional real estate interests can be in a condominium, town home, apartment, cabin, detached home, or hotel suite. Timeshare is typically a condo or hotel style of accommodation, offered in a developed destination resort.
- **Type of Unit** – The fractional residence typically reflects a second home with up to four bedrooms, roomy closets,

full kitchens, and comfortable living areas, although there are many timeshare properties that offer villa-style accommodations as well.

- **Owner Storage** – Fractionals and PRCs typically offer owners a secure on-site location to store personal items between visits; timeshares do not.
- **Service** – The level of personal service is much higher in fractional interests than with timeshare, typically including concierge service, valet, airport pick-up, and pre-arrival provisioning.
- **Ownership** – Fractional properties cater to an alternative "second home" market, with developers offering a "sense of worry-free ownership," while most timeshares offer a "worry-free vacation." Most fractional properties, like most timeshares, are deeded ownership.
- **Financing** – Fractional interests can typically be financed through lending institutions as a "second home" purchase, whereas the developer typically provides financing for timeshare purchases.
- **Price** – Fractional interests are typically more expensive than timeshare because of longer use rights, personalized service, amenities, and marketing as a second-home product.
- **Location** – The nature of the fractional interest is second-home ownership, so although they can be found in the same locations as timeshare developments, for example in Florida and California, they also occupy more diverse locations such as Montana, Minnesota, Oregon, and all high-end ski destinations. There is a recent trend towards fractional interests in high-priced urban locations such as New York, San Francisco, and London.

- **Exchange** – Both external exchange affiliates RCI and II, as well a several independents, include a luxury exchange program in their roster of services, offering an exchange network of luxury real estate assets in destinations around the world that are not available to timeshare owners.
- **Service Partners** – Many developers have added corporate partners to provide additional benefits to owners. For example, American Express, Mercedes-Benz, and NetJets are making certain programs available to Ritz-Carlton members.
- **Sales** – Timeshare is typically sold to the consumer by the developer sales team in a ninety-minute sales presentation. Fractional interests are sold much like a second home, with the buyer taking time to investigate and learn about the product and the development, often returning more than once before making a decision. Although both products are represented by a developer sales team, local realtor communities are typically active in the sales process of fractionals and PRC products, which is not the case in timeshare.

Let's apply the **Discovery Model** to the fractional interest industry.

### A Use Right

The designation for most fractionals and private residence clubs use rights is "shares." Traditionally, the use right is between two and twelve weeks of use. Typically, the developer removes anywhere from two to four weeks from the calendar for unit maintenance, repair or to free up more space available time, so the year may actually be forty-eight to fifty weeks, not fifty-two.

The common lexicon is:
- 1/4 share or quarter-share (twelve weeks)
- 1/6 share (eight weeks)
- 1/8 share (six weeks)
- 1/10 share (five weeks)
- 1/12 share (four weeks)
- 1/24 share (two weeks)

Fractionals are typically offered in larger blocks of time – 1/4 shares and 1/6 shares are common. Private residence clubs typically refer to "days" rather than "weeks," with twenty-one and twenty-eight days common. In theory, private residence clubs are for the use of the owners and as such, actual use can be "unlimited" and is only subject to use by other owners and the reservation policies.

**B** **Use System (typically)**
- Deed

Whether a fractional or a private residence club, both normally take the form of a deeded interest, consistent with most time-share developments in the U.S.
- Right-to-use
- Purchase contract
- Disclosure document
- Declaration of timesharing
- Estimated operating budget
- Covenants, conditions and restrictions (CC&Rs)
- Management rules and regulations
- Physical description

*To review the details of the use systems turn to pages 33-38.*

**C** **Use Management Plan (may include)**
**Reservation Systems**
1. Set calendar
2. Rotating calendar
3. Rotating priority
4. Rotating calendar with priority reservations
5. Open reservation system
6. Planned weeks with flex time

**Exchange System**
**Fees and Dues**
**Resort Management**

# RESERVATION SYSTEMS

Each development will have its own reservation plan that fits the location and use rights. Keep in mind that the use plans are created by the developer, so any/all of these plans can result in a unique hybrid. Most plans include space available for short getaways or off-season vacationing. Understanding the reservation system of a particular resort is essential to a good ownership experience.

### 1. Set Calendar
A set calendar is a system whereby owners have access to the property during the exact same period every year. For example, in a 1/4 share, where the use right is one week every month, one owner has the use right to the third week of every month (thereby guaranteeing Christmas week). This system is the least frequent among both fractionals and private residence clubs and most suitable for people who have very limited

flexibility or who simply want to use their vacation home at set times.

## 2. *Rotating Calendar*

One of the most popular reservation systems, which was initially created by Steve Dering in 1990, is the rotating calendar. It is a schedule that is established in advance and the use rights rotate forward each year. For example, in a 1/4 share, where the use right is one week every month, the first week of the month of the first year of ownership will rotate to the second week of the month in the second year and so on in perpetuity, to ensure all owners eventually receive every week of the year.

## 3. *Rotating Priority*

A rotating priority system offers all owners the opportunity to reserve some of their time within the "premium weeks," typically twelve months in advance. They are given the opportunity to put forward a first, second and third choice of dates during which they wish vacation in the course of the year. For example, in a 1/4 share, owner #1 has his first choice, Christmas. If Christmas is also the first choice of owner #2, he will get his second choice, Presidents' Week, instead. Owners #3 and #4 will have their first, second or third choices met, depending on availability. The following year, owner #1 goes to the end of the list, and owner #2 gets his first choice met, and so on. The system sounds more complicated than it actually is, and in most cases, owners get their first and second choices. Off-season or non-premium weeks are booked on a first-come first-served basis throughout the year, with access to all owners.

### 4. *Rotating Calendar with Priority Reservations*

The hybrid systems works by assigning "premium weeks" and holiday weeks on a perennial calendar, where owners receive "set" rotating weeks. For example, in a 1/4 share unit at a ski resort, Christmas week (and any other designated premium week) would rotate to each owner every four years. The rest of the year, reservations are made on a priority basis.

### 5. *Open Reservation System*

An open reservation system is just as it sounds, owners book on a first-come, first-served basis, typically twelve months in advance.

### 6. *Planned Weeks with Flex Time*

In this system, the owner is given all or part of his weeks as reserved time (either set or booked annually twelve months in advance) and the balance of use on a first-come, first-served reservation basis.

# EXCHANGE SYSTEM

### *Internal Exchange*

Due to the independent nature of the developments, internal exchange is not common in fractional interests, although some include more than one property, like Intrawest's "Storied Places" and DCP International's "Equity Private Residence Clubs." Most hospitality brands like St. Regis, Ritz-Carlton, and Grand Residences by Marriott have an internal exchange program within their club properties.

## External Exchange

A developer of a fractional product may get the opportunity to affiliate with an external exchange company if the resort meets amenity, room, resort, and service standards required by the exchange affiliate.

The quality, services, and amenities of fractional interests are much higher than in timeshare, and in an effort to exchange "like for like," a new category within the two largest timeshare exchange companies was developed. Group RCI offers the *The Registry Collection*® exchange program and Interval International offers *Preferred Residences*® exchange program to their affiliates. Intrawest has developed *Resort to Resort*® exchange program as a third option for developers.

---

### The Registry Collection

*The Registry Collection* program offers a luxury "leisure asset" exchange of more than 160 exclusive properties on five continents, including personal 24/7 concierge service, reservation consultants, and member discounts with partners providing luxury travel and services.

There is an annual membership fee plus additional transaction fees when using the exchange program, and membership is limited to developer affiliates.

www.theregistrycollection.com

---

### Preferred Residences

Through a joint venture with the Preferred Hotel Group, Interval International offers *Preferred Residences*, a hospitality branded membership and exchange program for luxury fractional resorts, private residence clubs, and condominium-style hotels. The program offers a fine collection of luxury exchange opportunities around the world, special privileges, and preferential pricing at participating Preferred Hotels and Resorts, a Priority Pass worldwide airport lounge program, a Hertz #1 Club Gold® membership, and personal concierge service.

There is an annual fee and additional transaction fees for using the exchange program. Membership is limited to developer affiliates.

www.preferredresidences.com

### Resort2Resort

*Resort2Resort* is an exclusive exchange network comprised of whole ownership, fractional, and condo hotel real estate developments at Intrawest resorts and a portfolio of selected partner resorts. Resort owners have access to a growing collection of more than two hundred properties at over forty-eight premier destinations around the world and access more than two thousand cruise itineraries with such leading cruise lines as Carnival, Holland America, and Royal Caribbean. There is an annual fee and additional transaction fees for using the exchange program, and membership is limited to developer affiliates.

www.resort2resort.com

> **The Elite Alliance**
>
> The principals of DCP International (DCP), the same group who established the country's first equity club at Deer Valley Resort in Park City, Utah in 1992, developed *The Elite Alliance*. It is the only true high-end *PRC-only* exchange company and membership is limited to a select group of luxury private residence clubs. www.theelitealliance.com

## FEES AND DUES

There may be additional fees, dues, or charges when you purchase a fractional interest and they can include the following:

*Closing costs* – Since real estate is purchased, closing costs may apply.

*Maintenance/HOA fees* – Homeowner fees are annual dues paid for the general maintenance, upkeep and repair of the individual units, the common areas, and facilities, and can include staff salaries, supplies, legal/accounting services, insurance, utilities, and property management fees. When you purchase a unit, your contract will indicate your fees for the year, listed in monthly or quarterly increments. Your contract should also include how much of a fee increase is permitted annually. A small resort with only a pool will be charging less in HOA fees than one with underground parking, owner's clubs, hot tubs, expensive furnishings, or such extensive personal services as concierge, pre-arrival provisioning, and valet service. HOA fees typically range from $250 to $1,300 *per week* for fractionals and from $1,400 to $2,100 *per week*[3] for private residence clubs, depending on ownership ratio, square footage of the residence, amenities and services.

*Special Assessment* – This is a clause in the purchase contract that outlines the financial responsibility of every owner to pay a proportional share, should something extraordinary occur that is not covered by insurance or if, for instance, the prices of utilities soar beyond what can be covered by the annual budget. Repair of a roof that was damaged in a storm, for example, could fall under "special assessment."

*Exchange Fees* – The external exchange company will have an annual membership fee as well as daily fees for domestic or international exchange. Typically, there are no annual fees for an internal exchange.

*Additional Fees* – Owners can incur a charge on a per-use basis, which is due upon check-out on each visit. Expenses vary by resort, based on services and policies, but commonly include long-distance calls, pre-arrival grocery services, room service, transportation, housekeeping, and gratuities.

*Property Tax* – Since these are deeded properties, there will be a property tax borne by the owner, associated with the share interest. Some management firms will include it in the monthly HOA fees, some will send the bill they receive to you, others will have the county send the bill directly. Make sure to ask how the property tax is set up, so that you understand how the bill is to be paid.


# RESORT MANAGEMENT

The management company holds the key, literally and figuratively, to the resort, maintaining its value, both in owner experience and in real estate. Property management firms control operating budgets, housekeeping and maintenance operations, staffing requirements, and management, as well as general day-to-day operations. They also may manage member services, which include reservations and exchanges, rental programs, and owner concerns and complaints. Without the management company, a resort would descend into chaos.

However, not all property management firms are created equal. It is extremely important that the property management firm for any resort have a history of excellent performance, a good inventory of resorts that are well run, and an arsenal of existing owners that are satisfied with the operations and the company. A fiscally responsible, well-run development that is pristine at all times, organized and run by happy, accommodating, professional staff members can make the ownership experience great.

The Home Owner's Association (HOA) board typically acts as a liaison between property management the individual owners.

## Fractional Interest Industry: Private Residence Clubs (PRCs) and Fractionals

### Similarities

- Step into any Discovery Gallery, read any postcard or brochure, and go onto any Web site that offers fractionals or PRCs for sale, and you will notice the developers are marketing and selling properties as alternatives to second-home ownership. The residences are comparable to expensive second homes, without the upkeep and maintenance worries of a second home, while paying a fraction of the cost of a whole ownership.

- The buyer motivation for most people who purchase a fractional interest is *loyalty to the area*. People want to be in a specific place, whether it is their favorite ski resort, a golf course, an ocean, or a chosen lake. They have a love for the area, take their families there as often as they can and would like to build a family "legacy" in that place.
- Both fractionals and PRCs appeal to the affluent and well traveled who expect exclusivity, full appointments, fine furnishings, and professional interior design in their choice of second home.
- Fractional developers spend an inordinate amount of time and energy on architectural details, both inside and out. Defining a sense of place and a sense of arrival to enhance the ownership experience is as important as service and amenities. The caliber and craftsmanship of the exteriors of the development tends to reflect grandeur or grace and is a large part of why people purchase fractional interests. Often a large, protective porte cochere with an attending valet is the first welcome for owners. Authentic, indigenous, and comfortably sophisticated living environments are what the best developers strive for.
- Fractional developments typically offer spacious luxury residences ranging in size from studio to four bedrooms. Most interiors have had the benefit of superbly talented designers. Whether the rooms are classic and polished or rustically elegant, they will take on the charm of the resort area or urban location. Whatever the style, every attention is paid to the smallest detail. Pillows are perfect. Duvets, divine. Art, authentic. Standard features may include exceptional local art and craft accents, antiques or local pieces of well-crafted furniture,

sub-zero refrigerators, granite countertops, and luxury electronics such as plasma televisions. In the bedrooms, designer duvet covers, luxurious down pillows, and custom bedding packages are generally standard. Bathrooms are never overlooked and often feature jetted tubs, multi-head showers, high-end fixtures, granite or tile countertops, along with all the small touches like deep, soft towels and pristine porcelain.

- In the United States, both fractionals and PRCs offer deeded ownership and title insurance. Like any other form of real estate, the deed can be sold, willed or transferred by the owner at any time. If a fractional interest property is offered outside the United States, or in a metropolitan area within the United States, typically a right-to-use regime is utilized.

- Services and amenities are consistent with a four or five-star hotel, with concierge service, housekeeping, front desk, valet parking, swimming pool, and fitness facilities.

- To increase the feel of a second home and to add value to ownership, flexible-use plans incorporate space-available and short-notice weekend booking programs.

- Bank or institutional financing is available for most types of fractional interests, whether they are a fractional or a PRC. Developers typically pre-select a lender that is familiar with the project to provide consumer financing, if required.

- Member services personnel play an important role in owner satisfaction. Many owners have an intimate relationship with member services and use them to facilitate reservations, bookings and departures, trouble-shooting, and so on.

- Owner's clubs have become an important part of shared ownership. By creating a place where owners can relax with other owners, meet friends, enjoy the game on a giant-screen TV, host a large family gathering, or kick back and play pool, developers have added another exclusive element to ownership.
- There is an onsite management element whether it is 24-hour front desk service or full concierge service.
- When an external exchange affiliation is offered, fractionals and PRCs have a separate and more exclusive choice of accommodation than timeshare. The exchange is for the category of luxury vacation residences.
- A board of directors of an HOA represents owners.
- In addition to the new resort developments that are coming onto the market, there is now an active re-sale market for both fractionals and private residence clubs.

We've had a look at the similarities between fractionals and private residence clubs, now let's examine the characteristics of each.

## Fractionals
## Location, Size of Share, and Price.

Even though "less expensive" is a relative term when used to describe exclusive resort real estate, fractional developments are typically located on land parcels that are less expensive for the developer to purchase and build on (e.g. ranch land, lakes, smaller ski resorts), or they are located within expensive resort areas but outside the reach of extraordinary high real estate prices (e.g. not ski-in ski-out locations but rather a short shuttle ride to the ski resort).

Share offerings are 1/4 share (twelve weeks), 1/6 share (eight weeks) and 1/8 share (six weeks), 1/13 (four weeks), and 1/17 (three weeks) with offerings in each resort corresponding to the demand in the marketplace, buyer use patterns, and market value for real estate in the area. (There may be some discrepancy between the weeks and share size for a particular resort because developers may remove from one to four weeks from the calendar for annual unit maintenance and it will reflect in the share size).

The price for fractionals will be set according to the location, amenities, and service level.

**Value Proposition.** A property sold as a fractional should have a good value proposition for a particular family. The property should be competitive with comparable second-home prices in the area. Amenities and services should closely complement the owner's needs and expectations. The share size should reflect the use needs or, in other words, how much time the average owner will use the residence. The HOA fees should be compatible with the service and amenities provided.

If there are too many weeks allocated and the resort is not convenient to get to, or the HOA fees are too high for the amenities and services offered, or programs are not compatible with use (such as rental programs), then owners can become burdened by the ownership. The good news is, however, there are usually more than one fractional development to choose from in every resort area, so finding the one that fits should not be that hard to do.

**Configuration.** Fractionals can be a condominium, apartment, townhome, cabin, or hotel suite.

**Service and Amenities.** One of the most pleasant aspects of ownership is the relationships that are formed with the service staff and management. In most well-run resorts, the valet, concierge, and management staff will know an owner family by name, will know where they are from, what they like to do, and where they like to eat. There is always a warm "welcome home" and a reunion-like atmosphere.

The most common amenities are swimming pools, fitness facilities, concierge or front-desk services and, of course, daily housekeeping. Remember, the more services and amenities a resort offers, the higher the annual maintenance fees will be.

**Rental.** With longer use rights, many resort properties offer a managed rental program to owners when they are not using the vacation home. Rental agreements are made on an individual basis with the property management firm and are never offered as a rental pool. ("Rental pools" are situations where everyone in the group gets an equitable share of the revenue). Typically, the management firm will receive at least 50 percent of the rental revenue. Owners can rent out the unit themselves (and keep all the rental revenue) if they wish, but they will be responsible for housekeeping, handling the reservations, issuing keys, and so on. Most owners find it more convenient to use the property management firm that is in place.

**Exchange Opportunities.** Most fractional properties are built by independent developers who offer an external exchange affiliate, like Group RCI's *The Registry Collection*® program or Interval International's *Preferred Residences*® exchange program, to enhance ownership and expand the vacation opportunities of owners. Fees will apply to this membership.

**Maintenance (HOA) Fees**. Fees are based on the cost to maintain, repair, replace, and service the individual units as well as the common areas of the resort and the grounds. The fees are also based on services extended to the owners.

For example, the wages of the concierge, valets, housekeepers, maintenance staff, and membership services are all part of the maintenance fees (also called the homeowners association fees). Fees that go into a reserve fund (to accommodate extraordinary repair or replacement) are also collected under this heading. The more services and amenities the resort offers, the higher the monthly maintenance fees will be. Maintenance fees are typically billed to the owners annually, quarterly, or monthly. Property tax may or may not be included. A prospective buyer should ask for and receive a copy of the operating budget for review before purchase.

**Storage.** Typically, secure owner storage ranges from an owner's "closet" within the residence to a secure onsite storage area. Owners often keep recreational equipment like skis, seasonal clothing, staples, and personal items that make their stay comfortable and vacationing more convenient.

**Additional Fees**. Additional fees may apply to any service offered, such as additional housekeeping, program fees, membership to the external exchange partner, and so on.

**The Big Why.** What is the buyer motivation for a fractional? Initially, it is not the concept. Very few people start out looking for a fractional property. Typically, they have been visiting the area for many years and expect to continue for many more. They may have been looking in the area to purchase a second home or they may have been staying in a resort that offers a fractional product. Whichever the scenario, they first love the area or region, then the resort, then the location of the resort, then the accommodations, and finally the amenities, management, management plans, and programs. Then they must see benefit in the "value proposition."

Most families want "simplicity" to return to their vacation planning. They don't want to struggle with a variety of hotels each year, they don't want the "headaches" of second-home ownership, and they also may see the value in deeded ownership. Simply put, they want to return year after year to a place that's theirs, to enjoy themselves, build family bonds, and perhaps leave a legacy property for future generations.

## Case Studies

Let's take a look at two examples of fractional properties. The properties offer a glimpse of the diversity of location, use rights, and management plans within the industry, and prove that there are no hard and fast rules to fractional developments.

The first, The Hammocks on Bald Head Island in North Carolina, is a beach retreat only accessible by a passenger-ferry ride from the mainland. The second, The Cottages at Cape Kiwanda, sits on a spectacular and coveted Pacific Ocean beachfront location in Oregon.

I am providing a direct reprint from a portion of their respective marketing material, so that you can experience part of the sales message, and then we will apply the Discovery Model to each.

## Case Study #1

The Hammocks *on Bald Head Island*
North Carolina
Bald Head Island is a beach retreat unlike any other. No bridge connects the island to the mainland, so travel to the island is limited to a 20-minute passenger-ferry ride or private boat. The absence of a bridge and cars serves to protect the island's relaxed pace and peaceful way of life. The Hammocks is a full-season resort neighborhood two miles off the southeast coast of North Carolina on a cape island that offers a staggering variety of environments – including ocean beach, tidal creeks and salt marshes, a maritime forest, a harbor and an 18-hole golf course – where 10,000 of the islands 12,000 total acres are forever set aside as a nature preserve. The separation from the mainland, and no vehicular traffic (ground speeds are as fast as the low-speed electric carts or your own two feet can carry you) add a psychological disconnect from the hectic pace of mainland living. On this very special island, relaxation and reconnection with nature and relationships are key. The summer months can be filled with nature hikes, canoe trips, strolling on the beach, and golfing. The semitropical climate permits golfing, fishing, hiking, biking, and relaxing outdoors even in the winter months.

### The Homes and the Neighborhood
The Hammocks neighborhood includes:
- Twenty-three homes, each professionally decorated and fully furnished, built around three landscaped courtyards
- Connecting boardwalks that link neighborhoods

- Homes with views of the golf course, the forest or the ocean
- Architecture that reflects traditional coastal Carolina elements, including wide porches, exposed beams, and cedar shingle siding
- Two-and three-bedroom floor plans
- Two master suites

## Ownership Opportunity
Hammocks owners enjoy four weeks of vacation time in their home every year.

## Reservation System
Each owner's week will move forward one week each year, ensuring that all owners will receive an equal opportunity to vacation during different times of the year and during various holidays.

## Services and Amenities
Owners have a year-round membership in three island clubs (owners get to enjoy the clubs even if they are not staying in their home):

*Hammocks Club* offers an onsite clubhouse, fitness room, games room with billiards and WiFi, hot tub, sauna, and heated pool exclusively for members and member's guests.

*Bald Head Island Club* includes an 18-hole golf course, tennis, croquet, and dining.

The *Shoals Club* is an oceanfront venue providing fine and casual dining, pools, recreational programs for children and adults, and direct access to the beach.

The HOA fees include sports memberships for the BHI Club (value: $22,000) and the Shoals Club (value: $12,000) as well as a golf cart for the home and II membership for three years.

## On Site

The property manager/owner services coordinator oversees check-in/check-out services and offers a variety of on-island services such as reserving tee times, making dinner reservations, and arranging equipment rentals. The Hammocks is managed through an elected Hammocks Association Board of Directors in accordance with governing documents and is operated for the use, benefit and enjoyment of Hammocks owners, their families and guests.

## Exchange

Interval International is the external exchange affiliate. Owners may also exchange their Hammocks weeks with other Hammocks owners through II.

## Pricing

Two-bedroom homes from $104,900 to $129,000 with annual HOA fees (est) $5,468

Three-bedroom homes from $123,900 to $205,900 with annual HOA fees (est) $6,574

www.hammocksclub.com
For Hammocks disclaimer, see footnote chapter 3/4

Let's apply the Discovery Model to The Hammocks.

## A Use Right

Four weeks annual use right, one week in each season.

## B Use System

- Deeded 1/13 interest.
- All related legal documents including sales contract, CC&Rs, operating budget, rules and regulations, external exchange agreement, and so on.

## C Use Management Plan

**Reservation system:**

- Rotating calendar

**Rental program:**

- No internal property management rental program is offered

**External exchange program:**

- Interval International (additional fees apply)

**Internal exchange program:**

- None

**HOA fees paid quarterly and include:**

- All club memberships
- Lease and maintenance of a golf cart
- Housekeeping services
- Property management and services including front desk and concierge
- Property maintenance and reserve fund
- Insurance
- Property taxes

**Property Management:**

Bald Head Island Ltd.

# Case Study #2

The Cottages at Cape Kiwanda
Pacific City, Oregon

The Cottages at Cape Kiwanda are beachfront properties overlooking the Pacific Ocean, with spectacular views of Haystack Rock and Cape Kiwanda. Located between Tillamook and Lincoln City, the Cottages are less than two hours from Portland, just off Highway 101 on the Three Capes Scenic Route. With unobstructed ocean views and the beach just steps away, the Oregon coast experience doesn't get any better than this. The nearby coastal town of Pacific City offers quaint restaurants, shops, and unique places to explore.

**The Homes and the Neighbors:**
- Eighteen cottages, luxuriously furnished, with relaxation and comfort in mind; neighbors mostly have fins or wings.
- Unobstructed ocean view and access
- Two and three-bedroom floor plans
- Private outdoor balconies and terraces
- Full kitchens with stainless-steel appliances
- Natural-slate entryways
- Flat-screen TVs, DVD players, and game systems
- Gas fireplaces, cook ranges, and barbeques
- Fine linens on king and queen beds
- Heated-slate bathroom floors
- Private, covered parking

## Ownership and Use

Sold in three-week fractional shares, these oceanfront cottages allow you to own on the coast at an affordable price, but without the hassles that normally come with a second home.

At the time of purchase, the unit you choose is the same unit you would always come back to. Owners have one primary fixed week in the high season, with the other two weeks in mid-and winter-season scheduled annually with priority choices for those weeks on a rotating basis.

## Services

- A professional management team takes care of every detail, from maintenance and housekeeping to concierge service.
- Trade your weeks with Interval International.
- Rental program.

## Pricing

| | Price Range | Homeowner fees (est. annual) |
|---|---|---|
| Two Bedroom (2 bath) – lower /upper (1/17th share) (approximately 985 square feet) | $79,900 – $92,295 | $2,810 |
| Three Bedroom (2 bath) – lower/upper (1/17th share) (approximately 1,150 square feet) | $102,398 – $113,295 | $3,255 |

Three Bedroom Grand
(2 bath) – lower/upper (1/17<sup>th</sup>)     $133,148 – $144,795   $3,692
(approximately 1,350 square feet)

> www.kiwandacottages.com
> For the Cottages at Cape Kiwanda disclaimer see footnote chapter 3/5

Let's apply the Discovery Model to the Cottages at Cape Kiwanda.

### **A** Use Right
Three weeks annual use right (one week at a time, three different times of the year.) Owners stay in the residence they purchased.

### **B** Use System
- Deeded 1/17 interest in a fixed unit.
- All related legal documents including sales contract, CC&Rs, operating budget, rules and regulations, external exchange agreement and so on.

### **C** Use Management Plan
**Reservation System:**
- One fixed week in high season
- Rotating priority for the other two weeks in mid and winter-seasons

**Rental Program:**

Owners who wish to rent part or all of one or more weeks may utilize Kiwanda Hospitality Group's Rental Program, can rent it themselves or may use an independent rental agency.

Kiwanda Hospitalty Group's Rental Program Guidelines:

- Owner may rent less than a full week
- Owner must give thirty days notice to Rental Manager
- Rental Manager sets rental rates and may offer special rates for marketing purposes
- Owner's HOA fees must be current to receive rental income
- Rental income paid out to owners twice annually
- Rental fee is 45 percent of gross rent

**External Exchange:**
Interval International

**Internal Exchange:**
None

**Property Management:**
Kiwanda Hospitality Group

## Private Residence Clubs (PRCs)

I am a consultant to AZUL Hospitality Group, a management and development company specializing in full-service hotels and upscale resorts headquartered in San Diego, California. Often we are asked to review a property that a developer has, with the intent of selling it as a PRC. Last year, Jeff Zogg (VP of the Condominium and Fractional Division) and I went to look at a property in Laughlin, Nevada. The developer wanted to know if the property he was planning to build could be sold as a private residence club. When we arrived, we scouted the "strip" and although it's not Las Vegas, it had its own charm. The property was on the "other" side of the river, that is, not on the casino side of town. Since the real estate mantra is still, "location, location, location" it worried us a little. We met with the developer and walked the property, which was located right on the river. The views were terrific, and a private pier extended into the river for water taxi pick-up and drop-off. A nice little island was just offshore of the property. Phase one of the development, a contemporary, well-built, and beautifully furnished condominium residence building had already been completed and sold as whole ownership. Jeff and I were sure the developer could deliver a private residence product, because the first phase met the architectural and building standards for a PRC. There were many great things about the property, but surrounding it were old homes, apartment buildings, gravel roads, and garbage bins. The entrance to the proposed development passed between rows and rows of large metal boat storage units, which the owners in phase one used to store their large boats. There were other concerns we had for this development to be sold as a private residence club, but the location itself removed it from the category. The developer had success selling the first phase of his project as whole ownership, because the project had been designed to accommodate the family who either wanted to live there full time, owned a boat, or for families who used it as a second home, and the price seemed to be perfect for his market. The owners could store their boats on site, they didn't want to be on the casino side but still had direct access to the water, and the entrance to the property was not a concern. We ended up recommending that he continue to sell phase two of his development as whole ownership, and knew with the history of a successful sellout of the first phase, that he would do well. Even though many developers are struck with idea of turning their next project into a private residence club, the attention to detail, provision

of services, quality of the residences, delivery of amenities, and location eliminate more projects than get the
green light.

**Exclusivity.** The most marked characteristic of a
private residence club is the exclusivity of ownership and
membership in a luxury-tier real estate offering. Owners are
typically called "Members" with a capital "M" and the club is
for the use of Members and their guests. In its "purest" form,
the private residence club does not provide a managed rental
program. If a vacancy occurs, other members are given the
opportunity to use the residence. It allows greater value and
flexibility to the membership as well as limiting access to the
renting public. However, every PRC creates its own management use plan, and some PRCs do offer a rental program.

**Services and Amenities.** If exclusivity is the distinctive
feature of private residence clubs, service is their calling card.
All PRCs pride themselves on their professional dedicated staff
with almost all offering 24-hour concierge service and once if
not twice-daily housekeeping. The trait that distinguished
PRCs from fractionals in the formative years, pre-arrival provisioning (i.e. placing personal items and supplies into the unit
before the owner arrives), still plays a prominent role in ready-
ing the residence for the member's arrival. As if for a stage
play, personal items removed from storage are placed in the
appropriate spots throughout the residence. Framed family
photos placed on the bedside table, a favorite cashmere blanket
draped over a deep, cozy chair in the living room, favorite
wines placed in the wine rack or chilling in the refrigerator –
it's all just part of the service. The clothing that was pre-sent is
pressed, cleaned, and hung in the master suite. It is customary
for staff to fill the refrigerator with favorite foods and bever-
ages. The effect of this staging completes the comfort level the

member expects from a second home. Naturally, event tickets, restaurant reservations, a private chef, and transportation are all just a request away.

Amenities often include a well-appointed owner's club or private member's lounge, a swimming pool, spas, and fitness facilities, as well as secure member storage.

**Brand Power.** Prestigious hotel brands such as Ritz-Carlton, St. Regis, and Fairmont have entered the private residence club market. These companies have strong histories of excellent management, superb service, and solid reputations within the luxury travel industry. There is a *cachet* to each of the brands in the hospitality industry that has translated well to shared ownership/use in the form of private residence clubs.

**Size of Share, Location and Price.** Share size offering for PRCs are typically 1/8, 1/10, 1/12, 1/16 in resort areas, with the 1/24 interest offered in exclusive metropolitan or "rare air" locations. The use typically extends beyond the share offering, with most reservation plans allowing liberal short-term, weekend, and space-available policies to accommodate the owners. Compared to fractionals, private residence club shares are much more expensive per square foot.[6] One reason is that PRCs are typically built in areas where land prices are at a premium, construction costs are high, and there is a scarcity of land for developers to build on. The other reasons are the extensive services, amenities, and high quality finishes of the residences. Exclusivity is uppermost in a PRC.

**Maintenance Fees.** Along with a higher price and a higher level of service, PRCs also have higher HOA fees.

**Storage.** Secure personal owner storage is typically provided.

**Rental.** Due to the exclusive nature of membership, most PRCs do not offer a managed rental program, with owners reluctant to give non-members (or the general public) access. In addition to the elite nature of a PRC, owners are not as concerned about a revenue stream to offset their cost, as they are about the availability of short-notice reservations.

**Exchange Affiliation.** Less than half of PRCs have an external exchange affiliation.[7]

However, where there are external exchange affiliations, such luxury exchange networks as Group RCI's *The Registry Collection®* program or Interval International's *Preferred Residences®* program are typically used.

There are some brands, like Ritz-Carlton, Fairmont, and St. Regis, that offer an *internal exchange* within the "family" for added value and flexibility. There are a few clubs that are linked to an *internal network* within a group of PRCs, like *The Elite Alliance*, developments marketed by DCP International as part of the Equity Residence Club family.

**Additional Fees.** Additional fees may apply to any services offered.

**The Big Why.** What is the buyer motivation for a private residence club? Most people become owners of residence clubs, just as with fractionals, first and foremost because of the love of a particular area or region – a vacation spot they visit at least once or twice every year.

Buyers appreciate the intimate and prestigious nature of membership, and covet the great service extended in residence clubs. They appreciate the extraordinary quality of the resort and residences. Most people in this category can easily afford a second home but typically want the services and ease of a vacation experience as provided by a PRC. They see the value in deeded ownership, the exclusive use by members only, the on-site storage, and the liberal reservation systems allowing almost unlimited use.

## Case Studies

Let's take a look at two examples of private residence clubs. First, The Ritz-Carlton Club, Kapalua Bay, which is the first fractional offering in Hawaii, arguably one of the most sought-after locations in the world, Maui.

Second, we'll take a look at Meriwether Ranch in Montana, an unexpected jewel of a resort that sits comfortably in the middle of 750-acre ranch complete with a world-class trout stream.

As with the fractional interval examples, I am providing a direct reprint from a portion of the marketing material for the two PRC case studies, so that you can experience part of the sales message, and then we will apply the more pragmatic Discovery Model to each.

Before we delve into the case study of The Ritz-Carlton, there was a "stop the printing press moment." Ritz-Carlton just announced a new brand, the Ritz-Carlton Destination Club. The new name embraces the success of the existing Ritz-Carlton Club, which is a private residence club, and adds a points-based Portfolio Membership option to it.

This new model differentiates two options:
1) Home Club Membership, which is the current offering of the Private Residence Club.
2) Portfolio Membership, which allows Members to customize their vacations through a points-based currency.

There are two things to note in this new model. Even though the new club is called a "Destination Club," it does not conform to the model used by the Destination Club industry (as defined and outlined in the next chapter). Secondly, the ability for owners to purchase points is unique to Ritz-Carlton. There are no other private residence clubs that offer an additional points-based program.

This case study is included to illustrate that that if there is one thing that is absolute in the shared ownership/use industry, it is that is it is constantly evolving. This year, Ritz-Carlton created something new in the fractional industry. I am sure in the coming months and years, others will follow Ritz-Carlton's lead as well as add unique programs to their own offerings in an effort to satisfy the changing needs and desires of the vacationing public.

Regardless of the offering, however, the Discovery Model should continue to serve you well, in determining the best fit for your family within the resort real estate industry.

## Case Study #1

### The Ritz-Carlton Club and Residences, Kapalua Bay
### Kapalua Resort
### Maui

### The Destination

Located at the world-class Kapalua Resort in Maui, The Ritz-Carlton Club is sited on Hawaii's second largest island, overlooking what many consider the island's most picturesque beach. For beauty, elegance and tranquility, few places rival Kapalua Resort. Kapalua Resort is known for its

23,000 acres of legendary beauty, and the lifestyle includes access to world-class amenities, three white sand beaches, award-winning golf courses, and a new Adventure Center.

The secluded 24 acre oceanfront Ritz-Carlton Club and Residences (the Residences are whole ownership) property includes palm-lined pools connected by paved walkways that traverse manicured grounds. Year-round golf, long days on panoramic beaches and tropical trekking on the planned 100 miles of trails including coastal, equestrian, biking, hiking, and walking pathways are what many describe as "paradise."

**The Club Residences**
Each of the sixty-two Club Residences feature an open floor plan that affords stunning ocean and mountain views. Club Residences are luxuriously and fully furnished with island-inspired design elements, superb craftsmanship, fully equipped gourmet kitchens, designer bathrooms, state-of-the-art entertainment systems, full-size washer and dryer, high-speed Internet access, and spacious private lanais with scenic ocean views. Two- and three-bedroom residences range from 1,912 to 2,257 square feet.

**Amenities**
- Valet-attended garage parking
- 24-hour security
- The Spa at Kapalua, a 27,000 square foot world-class luxury spa and fitness facility

- Private residence entrance with individual elevator access
- Private member storage
- Kapalua Resort Membership privileges including:
  - o Golf: Kapalua is considered the #1 Golf Resort in Hawaii and is celebrated for its world-class, championship 18-hole layouts:
    - ➤ The Bay – home to the Kapalua LGPA Classic debuted in October 2008
    - ➤ The Plantation – host of The Mercedes-Benz Championship and the PGA Tour season opening event
  - o Recreation Area: Using the naturally contoured slope, this multi-level 8,500 square foot gathering place will be highlighted by a lagoon-style pool with cascading waterfalls and a full-service bar and grill.
  - o Kapalua Spa: The nearly 30,000 square foot destination spa features modern and ancient therapies incorporating island ingredients and water-oriented rituals.
  - o Beach Club: The 6,100 square-foot club features a swimming pool and a member's-only bar designed for residents to relax and enjoy Kapalua's tranquility.
  - o Kapalua Adventure Center: The new home of the resort's activity offerings including the Mountain Outpost. Designed for exhilaration and education, the Mountain Outpost features eight dual-track zip lines that take riders over ridges and ravines, three suspension bridges, a 35-foot tall climbing tower, and a high ropes challenge course. Experience

the resort's natural scenery by exploring the new mountainside hiking trails. Kapalua Adventure Center will be the new home of the resort's activity Annual Signature Events: Celebration of the Arts, Kapalua Wine & Food Festival, and Whale Quest Kapalua.

## Services

- Club Members will be Members of The Kapalua Club, enjoying exclusive access to the private beach Club, the pool, grill and bar, and privileged access to the new Spa. Golf benefits include access to the three clubs as well as cart-fee-only play and advanced tee times at the Bay and Plantation Courses.
- Dedicated personal concierge
- Twice-daily housekeeping
- Airport pick-up
- Valet parking
- Pre-arrival provisioning
- Unpacking and pressing pre-sent garments
- Arranging complete itinerary
- Personal items placed
- Private catering on request

## Reservation System
### 1) Home Club Membership

The unique reservation plan is based on a 36-week calendar. That leaves 16 weeks of floating inventory per residence, which allows almost unlimited access to owners for the space available program.

To enhance program flexibility, owners have reciprocity access to other Clubs for exchanges as well as the opportunity to convert their allocation into an extensive Ritz Carlton Destination Club portfolio of residences, which include more than 80 affiliated hotels world-wide.

There are three basic reservation plans with associated benefits and are allocated to Members in a specific residence:

**Plan #1:**

**Ka-Papa** – Consecutive fixed week: 21 consecutive days that are fixed.

**Plan #2:**

Fixed and Float – 14 fixed days and 7 float days.

**Plan #3:**

Fixed and Rotating Float – 14 fixed days and 7 rotating float days.

## Space Available

- This program is based on a first-come, first-served basis and may be booked at any time, 60 days in advance of the request. Additional fees apply.

2) **Portfolio Membership**

    Reservations are taken on a first-come, first-served basis and is based on reservation procedures and availability.

## Internal Exchange

### 1) Home Club Membership

There is an internal exchange program with other Ritz-Carlton Destination Club properties, based on the reservation program. This use right is included within the 21-day use interest and includes reciprocal use at:

Ritz-Carlton Club, Aspen, Highlands, Colorado
Ritz-Carlton Club, St. Thomas, U.S. V. I.

Ritz-Carlton Club, Jupiter, Florida
Ritz-Carlton Club, Bachelor Gulch, Colorado
Ritz-Carlton Club, San Francisco, California
Ritz-Carlton Club, North Lake Tahoe, California
Ritz-Carlton Club, Vail, Colorado
Ritz-Carlton Club, Kauai Lagoons, Hawaii
Ritz-Carlton Club, Abaco, The Bahamas

## 2) Portfolio Membership

Use up to 25 percent of points for stays at 71 (out of 72) participating Ritz-Carlton hotels and resorts with the balance used for stays at the Ritz-Carlton Destination Club locations.

## Pricing

1) **Home Club Membership:** Pricing starts at $350,000 per deeded interest.

2) **Portfolio Membership:** Beneficial interests are sold in increments of 2,500 Club points with a minimum purchase requirement of 5,000 points. Pricing starts at $130,000.

www.ritzcarltondestinationclub.com
Ritz-Carlton disclaimer see footnote chapter 3/8

Let's apply the Discovery Model to the Home Club Membership and the Portfolio Membership, The Ritz-Carlton Destination Club, Kapalua Bay.

**A** **Use Right**
**Home Club Membership**
- 21 days
**Portfolio Membership**

- Dependent on points purchased

**B** **Use System**

**Home Club Membership**

- Deeded ownership 1/12 interest in a specific property based on 36 annual weeks
- All related legal documents including sales contract, CC&Rs, operating budget, rules and regulations, annual dues, and so on.

**Portfolio Membership**

- Beneficial interest in a trust
- Annual dues

**C** **Use Management Plan**

**Home Club Membership**

**Reservation System:**

- Fixed week
- Floating week
- Consecutive fixed week
- Space available per diem program (additional fees apply)

**Rental Program:**

No managed rental program.

**Services:**

Pre-provisioning

Housekeeping

Airport pick-up

Dedicated concierge

Personal chef at request (at most properties)

**Internal Exchange:**

Currently owners can make an exchange with other Ritz-Carlton Destination Club properties. Up to an additional fourteen nights can be used to convert to points and used within the portfolio membership inventory. Additional fees may apply.

**Property Management:**
The Ritz-Carlton Hotel Company, LLC

**Portfolio Membership**
**Reservation System:** First-come, first-served based on availability of travel dates and residence floor plan.

**Rental Program:** None
**Services:**
Housekeeping
Concierge

**Internal Exchange:** There is no internal exchange per se, as the points-based program is solely based on the exchange system. Members may use up to 25 percent of their points for stays at 71 (out of 72) participating Ritz-Carlton hotels and resorts, and the balance of their points at one of the Ritz-Carlton Destination Club locations.

**Property Management:**
The Ritz-Carlton Hotel Company, LLC

To illustrate the diversity within the private residence club category, let's take a look at the second case study in Montana, a sportsman's and outdoor enthusiast's paradise.

# Case Study #2

## Meriwether Ranch, Private Residence Club
## Melrose, Montana

Tucked among the cottonwood willows of the Three Channels section of Montana's Big Hole River 30 miles north of Dillon and 30 miles south of Butte, Meriwether Ranch is comprised of 724 deeded acres and nearly 100,000 acres of permitted land. Situated in the Big Hole Valley between the Tobacco Root Range of the Rocky Mountains to the east and the Pioneer Range to the west, the Beaverhead-Deerlodge National Forest abuts the western edge of the ranch, offering 3.32 million acres of accessible national forest lands for recreation. There is a wide variety of things to do in this genuine Montana setting, beginning perhaps with blue-ribbon trout fishing on the Big Hole, Beaverhead, Madison, Missouri and other nearby rivers and hunting for upland birds, waterfowl and big game. There is riding or hiking the trails of the nearby Beaverhead-Deerlodge National Forest; high-country trail rides and pack trips with half and full-day trips and riding lessons available at Meriwether Ranch and Canyon Creek Guest Ranch. There are historical tours of Nez Perce battlefields, Lewis and Clark sites, gold and copper mines and ghost towns; and for the golf enthusiast, the Jack Nicklaus Signature Old World course in historic Anaconda. In the winter months, the ranch is located within easy reach for downhill and cross-country skiing. Fine dining, antique shops, galleries, and western wear shops are nearby in Twin Bridges, Dillon, or Butte.

## The Residences

Meriwether Ranch is designed for the avid outdoorsman and offers two distinct residences: the Riverfront and the Sportsman.

### The Riverfront

The Riverfront Residences front the river, curling around Wisdom Island on the banks of the Big Hole's West and Middle channels. Beautifully set on one acre the two-story, wood-and-rock lodges are almost 4,000 square feet, with four bedrooms, four-and-a-half baths, a 1,300 square-foot great room, fully equipped kitchen with circular-sawn fir flooring, and top-of-the-line appliances. There are four classic hewn-stone fireplaces in the residences, one in the great room, one in each of the master suites and one on the porch.

### The Sportsman

The Sportsman Residences are clustered around the Casting Pond, hiding behind a curtain of cottonwood willows, with their backyards tucked against the foothills. With 2,800 square feet on a single level, nine-foot ceilings and two master suites, they have a signature feature: more than 700 square feet of outdoor living space. Inside, the residences boast rich-rustic timber and stone, circular-sawn fir plank flooring and fully equipped kitchens with top-of-the-line appliances.

## Amenities

- Meriwether Lodge – Classic Western ranch house in design, with interiors of dark wood, rich leather, and authentic Montana appointments with an oversized river-rock fireplace with twin hearths, one for the inside lounge and one for the outside deck

- Crane Meadow Equestrian Center – Spacious indoor riding arena, 22-stall barn with full boarding and grooming, fully equipped tack rooms, outdoor corrals and riding arena, secure horse trailer and boat- storage areas
- Swimming pool
- Outdoor spa
- Fitness center
- Private bar
- Dining room
- Guest business center
- Conference facilities
- Concierge desk
- High-speed Internet service
- Secure perimeter fencing and state-of-the-art automatic gate system activated by the owner's in-car operator or by keypad
- Predetermined pet-friendly residences (with restrictions) and kennels
- Canyon Creek Guest Ranch – Among 500,000 acres of wild lands, the lodge and sleeping quarters date back to the 1950's and have been completely updated for maximum comfort. The experience includes alpine and lake fishing, guided big-game hunting, horse-pack trips, chuck wagon dinners, nature tours and outdoor expeditions, and spectacular sightseeing and photographic opportunities. Hearty meals prepared by a full-time chef are included. Owners at Meriwether Ranch will have priority access to the ranch at discounted rates.

### Services and Privileges of Ownership

- Complimentary transportation to and from the Butte, Bozeman, Dillon, and Missoula airports
- Pre-arrival shopping for groceries and supplies
- Personal use of late-model SUV during your stay
- Concierge services for summer and winter activities
- Housekeeping
- Child and adult activities director
- Use of the ranch toys including mountain bikes, ATVs, snowshoes, snowmobiles, float-boats, etc.
- Personal storage facilities
- Maintenance and housekeeping of home, including deck and fire-pit
- Exclusive Meriwether Ranch travel agency services
- Four-star destination exchange program

### Unlimited Access

The reservation plan allows owners to make reservations – for either full or partial weeks – well in advance, for a guaranteed number of nights each year. A rotating priority reservations system, split-week, space-available reservation calendar, planned times, and reservation priority numbers are combined to create a unique reservation system for the greatest flexibility for owners allowing virtually unlimited access. Even though members own an interest in a specific property, the actual use of any one of the residences will be determined by the number of reservation requests combined with the number of residences available at any one time.

The Meriwether Ranch Private Residence Club is operated solely for the members and their guests.

## Pricing

Riverfront Residences (1/8 interest) 1st Release
$328,000 with estimated annual dues: $5,300
Sportsmen's Residences (1/20 interest)1st Release
$148,000 with estimated annual dues: $4,700

www.meriwetherranch.com

For  Meriwether Ranch disclaimer see footnote chapter 3/9

Let's apply the Discovery Model to Meriwether Ranch.

**A** **Use Right**
- Six weeks annual use right for the Riverfront Residences
- Two weeks annual use right for the Sportsman Residences

**B** **Use System**
- Deeded 1/8 interest in a Riverfront Residence
- Deeded 1/20 interest in a Sportsman Residence
- All related documentation including sales contracts, CC&Rs, operating budget, rules and regulations, external exchange agreement, and so on

**C** **Use Management Plan**
**Reservation System:**
- Rotating priority
- Split-week
- Space available

**Rental Program:**
None

**External Exchange:**
The Registry Collection

**Internal Exchange:**

None; however, owners do swap time.

**Property Management:**

Star Resort Group

# Summary

There are well over two hundred fractionals and private residence clubs in North America.[10] Each property is unique, but if you apply the Discovery Model as a starting point, you should be able to discover whether a property is a good fit for your family or not. Remember, too, that all documentation should be provided to you before you consider a purchase and should be reviewed by legal counsel.

### Questions You Should Ask to Find the Right Fit

- ✓ What are your vacation time needs?
  Does your family expect to vacation in the same place for a few weeks (or more) every year? Are you looking for two weeks a year or twelve weeks?

- ✓ What type of reservation plan fits your vacationing needs?
  Do you have flexibility in taking vacations or are your needs specific to certain times of the year, for example school holidays and Presidents' Week? You will want a set calendar if you need to vacation at the same time every year.

- ✓ Do the services meet your expectations?

- ✓ Do the amenities meet your expectations?

✓ Does the resort fulfill your leisure needs?
Are there activities and amenities in the resort or in the surrounding area that your family can enjoy – like a pool for the kids, or a ski slope, or an equestrian center? Perhaps you want to have a lake or ocean getaway place. Is there water access that allows water play and sports, or do you want motor craft or sailboat access?

✓ Is access to the resort convenient enough for your family? Share size and location go hand in hand. If you want to own a 1/4 share, for example, is the resort convenient enough to get to at least six to eight weeks of the year?

✓ Can you afford an increase in maintenance fees and property tax as well as any special assessment that may come up unexpectedly?
The HOA fees are established every year, although typically they cannot exceed a certain percentage increase annually. However, when the fees become a burden, the owner experience is diminished.

✓ How important is an external exchange affiliation to you?

✓ How important is a managed rental program?
If you are thinking about ownership in a resort that offers more use rights than you will use, how important is the potential revenue from a rental program for you? And if there *is* a rental program – how dependent are

you on the revenue, and what will happen if you don't get the projected revenue?

✓ Does the resort have the style and type of accommodation you are looking for, not just for now, but for years of family vacations?

## General Questions

❑ Is there a professional competent property management company that runs the resort?

❑ Who is the property management company? You should be able to ask other owners or go to the property management Web site to check their credentials. Have a look around the resort and pay special attention to the upkeep of the common areas, the general appearance of the resort and the attitude of the staff. Ask to meet the owner services manager.

❑ What is the operating budget for the development? Ask about any line item you don't understand or want further explanation about.

❑ What types of activities can owners participate in at no charge, or at discounted rates?

❑ What are the fees associated with all the programs? Is the fee structure transparent? For instance, space-available may have housekeeping fees attached to the program so you want to know what they will be. Ask about annual exchange membership fees and daily exchange fees.

❏ Are rentals permitted? Is there a rental agreement for owners with the property management firm? If the resort offers a managed rental program, ask what the policies are regarding rental service fees and how are they split between owner and management. What's the rental history of the type of unit you are considering, and what would the nightly charge be for your unit? How are the units rented out – on a rotation system or some other system?

❏ What is the process for selling the ownership interest? Are there any developer restrictions and do the services and programs transfer with the deed?

# ETC.

➤ Since this is a relatively new concept in the resort real estate industry, many new resorts are offering fractionals or private residence club real estate. If the resort is in the planning stages, the developer may offer a "reservation" program, where buyers are invited to put some money down (anywhere from $1,000 to $10,000 as a fully refundable deposit on demand) to become a "reservation holder." This entitles the prospective buyer to receive marketing information and allows the sales team an opportunity to provide the latest information possible to a client.

➢ If the developer is offering a "pre-sale" program, the prospective buyer typically puts 10 percent down on deposit to hold a unit, another 20 percent when a certain building benchmark is met, and then completes the sale when the developer has an occupancy permit. Pre-sale programs are very common, and serve both the developer and the buyer. The developer, of course, is getting a commitment and the buyer should be getting the best price, perhaps a choice of units and any "perks" that the developer offers for being the first to commit to the project.

➢ There are a few downsides to committing to a development that is not completed nor sold out. There will only be an estimation of both the annual homeowners budgets and rental revenues based on the property management's ability to forecast correctly as opposed to a historical reference; programs and services often change; and there may be delays in construction. As well, the developer (since he, in fact "owns" the units until they are sold) will run the homeowners association until the development is at least 50 percent sold and the owners can elect a new board.

➢ Since this is real estate, many deciding factors for pricing, sales and marketing strategies, services, and programs offered are dictated by the economy. In a buyers market, of course, they may be more incentives for a buyer to make the purchase. But if the development is located in a "rare air" location, or there is a pent up demand for resort real estate and the economy is doing well, it becomes a seller's market, and buyers consider themselves lucky to be able to buy a share in a great property that suits their vacationing needs.

➢ Each developer will include a disclaimer on promotional material. You should read the disclaimer presented on all material for a fuller understanding of the offering.

➢ In a new development, before the property is sold out, the developer retains the right to change any aspect of the management use plan including prices, programs, and service.

➢ The characteristics mentioned for typical fractionals and PRCs are simply a guide and overview. Many PRCs, for example, offer a managed rental program and many have an exchange affiliation. Many fractionals use the marketing position of "club" but offer 1/4 share ownership, and some fractionals are in ski-in ski-out locations. So, as with all things in shared ownership, it is best to discover the location, the amenities, and services that fit your needs and budget, and not worry whether the development is a private residence club or a fractional.

➢ Complete legal disclosures, legal definitions, obligations, terms, conditions, and so on should be presented to you in full and reviewed by legal counsel when you consider ownership in any project.

# 4

## Climb the Highest Peaks:
### *Destination Clubs*

> *"Twenty years from now you will be more disappointed
> by the things you didn't do than by the ones you
> did. So throw off the bowlines. Sail away from the
> safe harbor. Catch the trade winds in your sails."*

Mark Twain

## Introduction

As we climb up the mountain in the shared ownership/use luxury categories, it doesn't seem to get any headier than the newest entry into the marketplace. Destination clubs have received a lot of press recently, perhaps because the concept so epitomizes the ultimate in American dreaming. It provides a foundation for the quintessential luxury vacation experience – sophisticated, superb, and spacious residences in the most sought-after locations in the world, with an unparalleled caliber of personal concierge service.

This triangulation is setting a new standard in the luxury travel marketplace that's beginning to intrigue the affluent traveler.

Anyone who has seen the movie *Under The Tuscan Sun* was swept away by the bucolic beauty of the Tuscan countryside. Now members of Ultimate Escapes can vacation at Rico Salcio, a beautiful, exclusive and impeccably restored seventeenth-century farmhouse, situated high on a hillside on twenty private acres of Italian countryside in the town of Lucignano, the location for the movie.

We can all imagine ourselves recreating scenes from movies made in Tuscany – children playing, adults drinking the best local wines, great meals prepared with the freshest ingredients – and just for fun, let's include a private Italian Chef in pristine whites singing an Italian aria. Imagine your entire extended family sitting down to a late dinner under an overhang of bougainvillea, warmed by the most perfect weather and inspired by the most perfect views.

The "destinations" in destination clubs are imaginative, sought after, and in extraordinary locations around the globe. Homes in such world-class ski resorts as Telluride, Whistler, Deer Valley, Steamboat Springs, Lake Tahoe, and the French Alps; resort locations in Florida, Arizona, Colorado, California, South Carolina, Costa Rica, Mexico, Hawaii, Europe, and the Bahamas; spa resorts in California, Vermont, and the Turks and Caicos are only a few of the destinations members can access for their vacations.

If the pulse, shopping, arts, and culture of a vibrant world-class city are the experience members want, London, Paris, and New York are all just a reservation away. Perhaps, to quote John Updike, you are looking for the "historic fullness" of a city in Europe to explore, embrace, and experience. Locations in Italy, Spain, or France could be in the real estate portfolio.

For members of Ultimate Escapes, a stay in Paris, France, means opening the door to the 1,000 square-foot residence with two bedrooms, two bathrooms, and a newly remodeled kitchen. Located on a historic cobblestone street in a building that is more than two hundred years old, the residence is near the Centre Pompidou (Paris' Modern Art Museum) and just a stroll from such landmarks as the Seine river, Notre Dame, and the Louvre, a perfect glamorous, seductive, dream destination for any traveler.

Typically, destination club residences in resort locations are ultra-luxurious in size, furnishings, and amenities. Attention to the smallest details are never overlooked; even the Monopoly game has all the pieces. Villas and ultra-luxury private homes often exceed $1 million to $3 million in value with 2,000 to 5,000 plus square feet of space. Some destination clubs offer a full range of homes in the $3 million to $5 million range. Clearly, destination clubs provide an exciting start to any vacation experience – fully equipped and beautifully furnished multi-million dollar homes in the most exciting and desirable destinations in the world.

Service and access may be equally compelling arguments for membership. Every destination club prides itself on service. Almost every club has a 24/7 concierge, personal travel planner, or "escape planner" to facilitate its member's every desire and need before they travel, while they vacation and after they return home. Transportation to and from the airport, pre-arrival stocking of the vacation home, a butler, nanny, or private chef don't even begin to cover it. Getting tickets to sold-out events, booking a deep-sea charter or a private jet, getting a reservation at a hot new restaurant when there are no reservations available seems to be what the personal concierge is all about. One Exclusive Resort Club member recalls that while he was on a romantic getaway to Paris with his wife, the concierge secured a set of the coveted tickets to the sold out semi-finals in the French Open.

Access to exclusive beach and swim clubs, golf courses, health clubs, and spas is part of moving the vacation experience from the fantastic to the sublime.

If you have ever watched the movie *Moonstruck*, (and if you haven't, close this book and go rent it), there is a scene in which Nicolas Cage's character professes his undying love for Cher's character, even though she is engaged to his brother. He is so smitten and dreamy that Cher slaps him across the face and yells, "Snap out of it!"

That's a little what we are going to do now. We've been in the "vapors" – that wonderful ambrosia of imagined sights and smells, making a mental list of places we would like to experience. Now that we are back on Earth, here are the nuts and bolts of destination clubs.

## Overview

The major selling point for destination clubs is the luxury vacation "experience." The differentiator between a luxury private residence club and the destination club is really about the needs and wants of the consumer. Luxury private residence clubs fit the family who wants to return (several weeks a year) to a specific location. They love skiing in Aspen, or they regularly spend time in San Francisco, or they want to return to their ranch home in Montana year after year and build a legacy of vacation memories with their family in a particular place they love. Occasionally, they want to travel to another destination and will use the "exchange" opportunity, but for the most part, they use the fractional or PRC as their second home.

Destination clubs, on the other hand, offer members experiential legacy vacations in "rare air" locations. These clubs appeal to families who want to explore the world, taste different cultures, take part in activities they have always dreamed about, explore the greatest resorts in the United States and abroad, but are not tied to one location. Destination clubs satisfy the wanderlust in all of us, albeit wanderlust in combination with the most sumptuous of accommodations.

Many people who consider a destination club also take advantage of the size and luxury of the club's real estate portfolio by traveling with a network of friends and extended family. They love the companionship and diversity of travel companions, always finding people in the group who want to explore and share in certain experiences during the day, take in eighteen holes, relax on the beach, stroll into town to poke about, and then meet up again for dinner.

Clubs of all price ranges are careful to stress they are "lifestyle" investments rather than real estate investments – even in those clubs that are structured for members to benefit from any appreciation of the real estate portfolio.

The destination club is still in its infancy, with an estimated membership base of 6,400[1] but the industry's optimism for growth could be realized as top clubs expand their offerings, hotel brands begin to enter the industry, and consumers become aware and more trustful of the industry.

## A Recent History of Destination Clubs

As happens most things that are new and untested, the first destination club, Private Retreats, later known as Tanner and Haley, filed for bankruptcy in 2006. Many questions were raised about the business model the club was based on and many agreed that although the model Tanner and Haley used was unsustainable, the concept was still viable. The early, flawed model, had promised 100 percent refunds of membership deposits, but more importantly, it guaranteed reservations whenever members requested them, even during peak holiday times. The club had to lease a lot of properties to accommodate demand – according to the Sherpa Report, Tanner and Haley was estimated to be leasing approximately 70 percent of its homes.[2] In December of 2006, the club was acquired by Ultimate Resort, providing relief to most of its members who eventually became members of Ultimate Resort.

In a show of continuing growth, in September of 2007 Ultimate Resort announced the $200 million merger with Private Escapes (the industry's third-largest destination club) to create the second-largest club in the industry, with 1,200 members and 140 residences in fifty destinations. The new club is called Ultimate Escapes and in November 2009, became the first publicly-traded luxury destination club in the world. Exclusive Resorts is the largest destination club, with over 3,000 members and more than 375 residences.

The clubs in active sales have learned from Tanner and Haley's unfortunate demise and are eager to point out how their operations are different from those that led to the bankruptcy.

Industry leaders Exclusive Resorts and Ultimate Escapes have been at the forefront of establishing formal industry-wide best practices, including limits on the proportion of properties a club leases (rather than owns) and requiring clubs to be able to have enough cash and assets on hand to fully back up member deposit refund requests.

Destination clubs today are more transparent in their business models. Almost all offer access to financial statements and have implemented various assurances and guarantees.

Nevertheless, consumers should ask to see adequate financial information and documentation demonstrating that a club can refund deposits as well as evidence that sales and marketing costs are not covered by the refundable portion of those deposits.

In addition, Adam Wegner, president of the Destination Club Association, says "The industry offers many choices, and a prospective member should, at a minimum, consider the following when deciding which destination club to join: the appeal of the club's portfolio of residences and destinations, the range of services and amenities offered, the importance of other club benefits (such as experiential travel opportunities), club fees and dues, existing club member satisfaction, the club's operational history and management team, and the overall financial stability and business growth model of the club."[3]

## What Is a Destination Club?

It is easier to understand the essence of the destination club concept, if you are familiar with a golf and country club. One of my favorite sports is golf. I love everything about the game. Pushing the small wood tee in the ground knowing that my shot may depend on the way it sits, hearing the "clink" when the club head meets the ball, driving around in that crazy little golf cart. I know, to someone who doesn't play (and for many who do), the emotional attachment is difficult to explain. What is even more difficult to explain is why people would pay huge amounts of money to join a private country club when there are perfectly good public courses in every town. I must admit, I am a public course person. But when the opportunity presents itself to play with someone who is a member of a country club, my heart races. There is something about a country club, maybe it's the exclusivity (you know, Woody Allen's great quote, "I wouldn't want to join a club that would have me as a member"), maybe it's the service, maybe it's just knowing that my friend invited me as a special treat. The destination club is a new luxury vacation alternative based on a country club model. It may sound like an indulgence, and it is. For folks who can afford to join a destination club, just remember, you can take guests!

Just like a country club, developers typically retain ownership or have the use rights in the real estate portfolio. A deposit refund mechanism is typical in most clubs and if a member resigns from the club, they typically receive a 75 percent to 80 percent refund of their initial deposit, although there are clubs that offer a 100 percent refund on the deposit after conditions are met.

One of the most interesting facets of this industry is the diversity between clubs. Each club has a unique membership use model, portfolio of homes, membership fee structure, resignation and refund policy, member-to-residence ratio, and financial accountability practices. Additionally, each club has a distinct marketing position, philosophy, and niche market. Clubs are individually designed to appeal to a particular lifestyle, income level, and vacation experience.

## Characteristics of a Destination Club

**The Residences.** The destination club has the most opulent, luxurious, and spacious accommodation real estate portfolio in the shared ownership/use industry. Residences are chosen for their size, finishes, furnishings, amenities, and, of course, location. Often these accommodations come in the form of private residences, villas, or, in urban locations, five-star hotels. The value of these homes ranges from the lower end of $1 million to close to $6 million each. The standards in choosing homes for the clubs are as rigorous as one might expect. Each club has its own standard for the style, amenities, size, and price of the residences, which makes it one of the differentiators to look for when choosing a destination club.

**The Locations.** The locations are undeniably in the most sought-after places in the world. Even within the prime locale, the residences are situated on prime real estate.

Some clubs have an extensive network of residences throughout the world, while others are designed to offer fewer locations but more prestigious homes.

The club model is designed for expansion, with most clubs constantly acquiring new residences in new locations. "In development" and "under construction" or "planned" are phrases typically used to describe the expanding real estate portfolio.

**Experiential Excursions and Member Events.** Adventure and excitement are all becoming part of the extraordinary menu of vacation options for club members. Exclusive Resorts, for example, offers "Once in a Lifetime Experiences." Members can reserve trips to take the family skiing in Patagonia, on an East African safari, biking in the Loire Valley, or to the Kingdom of Bhutan.

Many clubs now plan member events throughout the year. Exclusive Resorts families could spend time together enjoying a Harry Potter–inspired weekend at Bovey Castle in England, or participate in the Annual Member Golf Tournaments. Ultimate Escapes offers members experiences like fishing in a remote part of Costa Rica or guided climbing trips to Mount Kilimanjaro.

**The Services.** Without a doubt, the services offered in most destination clubs are as important as the residences and the locations. The typical 24/7 concierge service can include everything from vacation pre-planning, event and activity reservations, pre-arrival provisioning, and anything else a family needs to make their vacation experience pleasant and hassle-free.

**Membership Plans.** Some clubs have a membership model based on days of usage; for example, there is a fifteen-day or sixty-day (or anywhere in between) membership plan. Other clubs base their membership plans on home value. For example, homes in the $1 million, $2 million, and $3 million range. Still others may have only one plan with unlimited use. Each club membership model is unique to a particular club, so it is important to take a look at many clubs to ascertain which club may be a good fit for your family.

**Life of a Membership**. Some clubs offer perpetual memberships, which means that the membership transfers to another family member upon a member's death. Other clubs have a right-to-use model that limits the number of years the membership is active. Typically, in the right-to-use model, the membership reverts back to the club, and deposits (as stated in the refund policy) are refunded after thirty years.

**The Big Why.** People who choose a destination club membership typically have the resources to travel wherever they want to and stay in five-star accommodations. So why do they choose to join a club?

Most members see the value in the exclusivity of the residences – in most cases even five-star hotels and resorts cannot consistently provide the size of accommodations that are available in the real estate portfolio of a club. There is always enough room for family and friends, and most members enjoy being able to extend the gift of the vacation experience to others.

For many members, privacy also plays a large role in the value proposition. These residences offer families a chance to really unwind, explore, laugh, and get in each other's hair. Most resort homes have private outdoor areas, with some offering private swimming pools.

Service has been the enduring value as well. Families simply do not have to do any worrying, advance planning, or scheduling as they would normally do in planning several vacations a year on their own. They can choose the vacation experience they want, phone in a reservation, and – if it's available – pack their bags.

Some express that the best use of their prosperity is to share it with family and friends, and joining a destination club allows them the freedom and spacious accommodations to do just that.

Some folks even say the economics of a destination club make sense. The cost of owning and maintaining a second home or renting this type of accommodation with the service and amenities for several vacations a year, plus eating every meal out, may actually be higher.

## How Non-Equity Destination Clubs Differ from Timeshares, Fractionals, and Private Residence Clubs

➢ Members of non-equity clubs do not purchase real estate directly or indirectly.

> ➤ Members do not have communal rights, and there is no HOA.
> ➤ Members have the opportunity to receive a refund of a portion of the initial membership fee when they resign from the club, after conditions are met.
> ➤ There is no potential rental income from a destination club.
> ➤ There is not an external exchange element to destination clubs.
> ➤ There is no ability to store personal items due to the nature of the club's multiple locations.
> ➤ They are not regulated under same state timeshare laws.

Let's apply the Discovery Model to destination clubs.

## Discovery Model

### A Use Right

Although every club has a unique membership program, most clubs offer from fifteen to sixty days of annual reserved use. Plans vary, however, with some clubs offering, in addition to the reserved time, unlimited space-available days while other clubs limit the number of space-available days subject only to the reservation plans. There are also clubs that have plans for additional days (with associated fees) that are purchased on a one-time basis. There are clubs with unlimited usage (within the reservation policies) and only one membership plan.

### B Use System

Both equity and non-equity clubs are currently being offered in the marketplace, and the definitions of each are presented.

However, due to the overwhelming prevalence of non- equity clubs and the complex use system governing equity clubs, the application of the Discovery Model, subsequent information and examples apply only to non-equity clubs. It should be noted that, although the use system used to construct the equity club offering is different, the basic use right and management plan models still apply to equity clubs.

### Equity Clubs

Members of an equity club own a share in the limited liability company/partnership that owns the clubs and/or its properties. Since shares are issued and members receive registered securities, clubs need to comply with security laws. Such restrictions make it difficult to market the clubs, since potential members must be accredited investors. However, there are successful models that cap the fund's debt, keep the annual dues low, and close the fund after a certain number of years, selling the real estate, with the intent on returning the initial investment and a percentage of any real estate appreciation.

### Non-Equity Clubs

The most common structure among destination clubs by far is the non-equity club. Members do not have any equity or shareholder status in any real estate. Rather, the investors hold the deeds to all the properties in the club portfolio, so the equity remains with the investors. Members have the right to stay in the properties and use the services set out in the reservation systems, but they do not own any property nor benefit from appreciation of any real estate.

Much like a country club membership, an initial membership fee is paid, followed by annual dues. There can be "term" limits on club membership (for example thirty years), at which time the membership can be renewed or terminated with a refund, or the membership can be offered in perpetuity. Most clubs allow the transfer of a membership to an approved family member.

Since membership cannot be sold but only reassigned back to the club, destination club developers typically refund between 75 and 80 percent of the initial membership fee after conditions have been met.

Club members do not include their membership as part of their investment portfolio, but rather as an investment in their vacation experience.

### Membership Application
Before considering a membership, most clubs require a membership application to be filled out, with personal and financial information like bank records and references; some clubs even ask for a refundable deposit along with the application. The club reviews the application and, if accepted, will then execute a Membership Agreement.

## Membership Documents

### ❑ *Club Membership Agreement*
A binding contract between the club and the member, clearly indicating membership in the club. The contract typically includes the club's policies and may include obligations for payments, disclaimers for investments, reservation and use policies, security of member deposits, annual dues and general

payment policy, resignation policy, termination policy, transfer of membership policy, and regulatory risk, as well as any miscellaneous provisions made by the club.

❑ *Club Rules and Policies*

These are the written rules, regulations, and procedures that are adopted by the club to facilitate the policies and operations of the club; they may include reservation policies and procedures, disclaimers, force majeure, cancellation procedures, use of club vehicles, smoking, pets, house rules, maximum occupancy, additional fee schedule, annual dues procedures, and suspension or termination of privileges. The rules and policies are designed to protect the club's properties and the health and welfare of the members and their guests, and to keep the club running smoothly.

**C** Use Management Plan

*Membership Plans, Fees, and Dues*

The initial membership fees/deposits and annual dues vary widely from club to club, as illustrated in the examples below. Typically, each club offers a range of membership options within its club offering plan levels, providing fifteen to sixty days, holiday use and adding family members as designees. Clearly, each club is unique and designed to appeal to individual lifestyles, travel desires, and budgets. Membership fees will reflect the cost of the luxury level of the residences, locations, level of service, availability of homes, access to reservations, and most importantly, the commitment of the club in meeting its members' expectations.

For example:

➢ Exclusive Resorts offers six membership plans: 10, 20, 30, 40, 50, and 60 membership days, with fees from $139,000 to $479,000 and annual dues ranging from $13,900 to $59,000.*

➢ Ultimate Escapes offers three clubs (Premiere Club, Signature Club and Elite Club) and five membership plans (14, 21, 28, 42 and 60 membership days) with fees from $70,000 to $425,000 and annual dues ranging from $8,000 to $45,000.*

*All prices and plans are subject to change at any time.

### Additional Fees

Typically there are no additional fees for pre-trip planning, in-residence concierge, housekeeping services, or such on-site amenities such as private beach clubs and privileged resort access at most destinations. Fees may apply for additional days, extended family access or special programs, but each club sets its own policies and there are no standard practices.

### Member-to-Property Ratio and Occupancy Rate

A distinctive feature of destination clubs is the member-to-home ratio. In a private residence club, the share size – e.g., 1/6 – indicates there are six owners for one residence. In non-equity destination clubs, since the residences are not "owned" by the members, use is typically indicated by the member-to-home ratio, which typically ranges from 5:1 to 7:1, that is, five members to one home or seven members to one home, respectively. The number may always be in flux, as homes and members are continually added (and subtracted), but it gives the consumer an idea of how many members are going to be booking reservations. Clubs that have a 10:1 ratio, for example will have fewer opportunities for their members to book reservations than clubs with a 6:1 ratio.

The second factor is the occupancy rate. Clubs generally have an occupancy rate of between 50 and 70 percent, with occupancy rates higher during peak seasons.

Clubs must balance the number of homes in their real estate portfolio with their membership to ensure that their reservation and space-available plans meet member expectations.

### Reservation Systems

There are typically five reservation categories that may be incorporated to formulate the reservation system of a particular club:

1) Advance Reservations – This system allows members to make reservations in advance (typically twelve months to twenty-four months). The number of advance reservations that can be made depends on the type of membership that was purchased. Each club has a unique reservation plan with rules and guidelines for members.

2) Short Term – This system allows shorter time frames for booking a reservation.

3) Holiday/Peak Season Reservations – Most club plans have put these high- demand periods into a separate reservation/membership plan and provide a system for equitable opportunity within the plans. Some clubs use a rotating-priority system for holidays, some clubs place a limit on the nights spent during holiday seasons (e.g., fourteen nights during the year and seven nights during a holiday season) and so on.

4) Space Available – Useful for short-term and short-notice reservations, most clubs have a space-available program within the membership plans. Typically, reservations can be made between zero and ninety days before departure (sometimes longer) and can offer shorter stay periods. Some clubs count this as plan usage; other clubs do not.

5) Simultaneous Home Use Privileges – Members can make and use multiple reservations to use multiple homes in the same or different destinations at the same time.

## Resignation System
### Membership Deposit

Most clubs offer a 75 percent to 80 percent refund of the initial membership deposit after conditions are met. Some clubs offer a variable refund based on the number of years of membership, for example, 80 percent after the first year, 90 percent after the second year, and 100 percent after the third year. Others have a policy that a member must belong for one or two years before submitting a resignation request.

### In/Out or Exit Ratio

Most clubs operate with a resignation ratio, that is, a resigning member must wait for new members to join before receiving a refund on his or her initial membership deposit. The term for this is "in/out." For example, if the resignation ratio for a particular club is 3:1, it means that three members must join "in" before one member requesting "out" receive their deposit back.

It is important to understand the refund policy of any club you are considering joining, as there is no set industry standard.

Each club will have a policy regarding:

- The amount of the membership deposit refund
- What the exit ratio is before a refund can occur
- When the refund will be administered

### Financial Transparency

Most of the membership deposits received in a non-equity destination club are invested in real estate and are, therefore tied to real estate values. Typically, the security of membership deposits is initially dependent on the club's ability to re-market the membership at a higher value. If membership deposits cannot be re-marketed, the security of the deposits becomes dependent on the assets of the club.

In an effort to provide stronger guarantees and assurances to current and prospective members, destination clubs have made an effort to change or introduce changes to their business models that disclose the necessary financial information to show that club assets are sufficient to repay member deposits.

Some clubs bring in independent auditors to perform annual audits; some clubs provide their members detailed financial reports; and others provide an annual or semi-annual financial letter, confirming the deposits are covered. Some clubs have created a model whereby club properties are put into a legal entity held inside a members' trust, where members have preferred rights over unsecured creditors to assets in the trust. Some clubs also make guarantees about how member deposits are used. Exclusive Resorts and Ultimate Escapes pioneered the "Net Asset Test," a program designed to confirm that the value of assets can meet all obligations, including repaying all refundable membership deposits in accordance with their Club Membership Agreement. The club reports the results of the test calculation quarterly to their board, and annually to their members, and has become the standard by which most other non-equity destinations clubs report their financial situation. (Details on the "Net Asset Test" are included in the overview of Exclusive Resorts.)

However, in addition to financial transparency, it is important to stress that in an economy of decreasing real estate values, club debt, adding new members, and the solvency of existing members remains an important factor in determining the financial strength of any club.

### Services

One of the outstanding membership benefits in addition to luxury residences and spectacular locations is the service element in a destination club. Designed to meet the specific individual needs of its members, each club has a unique level of service, with most clubs providing pre and post-vacation planning, personal concierge or service planners 24/7, and on-site hosts. Many clubs offer a luxury vehicle at each location for the convenience of their members, airport transportation, and complimentary daily housekeeping.

### Added-Value Partnerships

Corporate partnerships vary from club to club and are incorporated to enhance membership. Exclusive Resorts, for example, has alliances with Best of the Best Services, Avis Chairman Club, Mayo Clinic Preferred Response, American Express Executive Travel Desk, and Marquis Jet. Ultimate Escapes offers club benefits including Bruce World of Travel, which provides customized tours with 24-hour notice, American Express Double Membership Reward benefits, and Bombardier Flexjet and Skyjet charter flights and jetcards.

## Destination Club Association

The destination club industry abides by consumer laws and FTC regulations but is not regulated by most states in the same way that timeshare and fractional/private residence clubs are. In 2006 the Destination Club Association (DCA) was formed under the leadership of Adam Wegner, Senior Vice President and General Counsel of Exclusive Resorts.

*Industry Best Practices* was adopted by the association and outlines the fundamental principles that guide the industry:
- Comprehensive consumer disclosures
- Accurate, truthful, and appropriate marketing and sales practices
- Financial responsibility
- Responsible industry growth

*Code of Responsible Business Conduct* (adopted in 2007) detail requirements and key provisions, which include:
- Member rescission rights
- Required club disclosures
- Financial responsibility – net asset test
- Prohibited acts
- Local operating requirements

## Case Studies

Let's look at the details of two non-equity destination clubs. The information is supplied by each club, and is included so that you can experience part of the sales message. The Discovery Model is applied on a chart at the end of the case study section.

The first is Exclusive Resorts, currently the largest club with 376 residences on 300 properties (166 more in development), in 35 destinations around the world, with more than 3,000 active members. The second club is Ultimate Escapes, the second-largest club, with a combined portfolio of 140 exclusive club properties in 50 global destinations, with 1,200 members.

Reviewing these clubs should provide a glimpse of the diversity of non-equity destination clubs.

## Case Study #1

**Exclusive Resorts**

Exclusive Resorts, the world's leading luxury destination club, combines the size and elegance of a private residence with the service and amenities of a luxury resort. Members pay a one-time Membership fee (the majority of which is refundable) and annual dues. With over 300 remarkable residences (and another 166 in development) thoughtfully spread among 35 of the world's most compelling destinations, the current 3,088 members make the world their second home. The beautifully appointed, spacious residences are valued at an average of more than $3 million each and include 24/7 personalized Onsite Concierge service and privileged access to resort amenities.

**Your Vacations Await**

Club residences are located in the best locations within each Destination – a short walk to the beach, ski-in/ski-out access, adjacent to the golf course or in the heart of the city.

**Beach:**

Laguna Beach, CA

Bonita Beach, FL

Ft. Lauderdale, FL*

Miami Beach, FL

Sea Island, GA*

Kapalua, HI*

Kohala Coast, Big Island, HI

Wailea, Maui, HI

Kiawah Island, SC

The Abaco Club, Bahamas

Little Dix Bay, A Rosewood Resort, British Virgin Islands

Anguilla, British West Indies*

Grand Cayman, Cayman Islands

Peninsula Papagayo, Costa Rica

Canouan Island, The Grenadines

Los Cabos, Mexico

Real del Mar, Puerto Vallarta, Mexico

Turks and Caicos

**Mountain:**

Lake Tahoe, CA

Snowmass, CO

Steamboat Springs, CO

Telluride, CO
Vail and Beaver Creek, CO
Deer Valley, UT
Jackson Hole, WY
Whistler, British Columbia, Canada
The French Alps, France
**Metropolitan**
San Francisco, CA
Chicago, IL*
Las Vegas, NV
New York, NY
London, England
Paris, France
Florence, Italy
**Leisure**
Scottsdale, AZ
Miraval, Life in Balance, Tucson, AZ
Carnegie Abbey Club, Newport, RI
Bovey Castle, Devon, England
Tuscany, Italy
Sailing aboard *The World*

*Under Construction


**Every House, a Home**

The residences in the real estate portfolio average 3,500 square feet of living space – ample room for big families and guests. Residences typically include "great" rooms, a wonderful place to gather and watch a movie or to play charades and spend time together, as well as significant outdoor space with private pools and hot tubs. But they also provide enough space to privately read a book or let the small ones (or Dad) take a nap before they play again. The homes offer state-of-the-art electronics like plasma televisions, sound systems, wireless Internet, and PlayStation video games. The chef-grade kitchens are well equipped with every possible necessity and a few surprising non-necessities as well. From fine linens and sumptuous bath towels to champagne flutes, the homes come totally equipped. The residences reflect world-class architecture, acclaimed interior design with touches of local artisan details reflected in each unique location. The metropolitan destinations have two bedrooms and are approximately 1,250 square feet, most with full kitchens and large living areas. From a glass tree house in Costa Rica to a modern beach home in Abaco, to a soaring ski chalet in Whistler, these homes set the stage for great vacation memories.

## Unique Privileges of Membership

Through the Club's amenity arrangements, Members have access to the services of an array of world-renowned five-star hotels, resorts, and private clubs.

## Service Redefined

Exclusive Resorts handles everything.

Services like daily housekeeping, dinner reservations and arranging transportation can be expected in any five-star luxury hotel. But club members can expect truly *personalized* service. Member Service Managers take care of all the planning aspects of a member's trip, including destination planning, vacation itineraries, and any personal assistance required. The on-site concierges are available 24/7 to manage all requests, including reserving a private chef, dinner and theater reservations, ground transportation, grocery shopping, and making spa appointments and, well, go ahead and make their day – suggest the impossible. Exclusive Resorts maintains a staff of local service professionals in each location to ensure superior service. Housekeeping naturally includes changing linens, washing the dishes, and generally keeping things tidy while members are having the time of their lives.

## Once in a Lifetime Experiences

Once in a Lifetime Experiences are designed to bring members closer to the people, culture and natural beauty of the world. The program for 2008/09 includes planned experiences in twenty-five countries on six continents. Exclusive Resorts did the homework, members need only go discover. Family-friendly journeys include Walt Disney World Resort adventures in Florida, a dude ranch experience in Western Ranch, Colorado, a family-friendly biking tour in the Loire Valley in France and, of course, Mediterranean cruises. Experiences designed to excite, challenge and inspire include a South African safari, an Antarctic expedition, family skiing in Patagonia, and biking in Provence, France. Not to let the romance get away, couples-only escapes have been readied in exotic hideaways around the globe. Refresh, relax, and rejuvenate in Le Sereno and Hotel Le Toiny in St. Barts, at the Six Senses in Koh Samui, Thailand, at the Wakaya Club in Fiji, or at Chateau Eza in the south of France.

# Membership Plans

| Membership Days | 10 | 20 | 30 | 40 | 50 | 60 |
|---|---|---|---|---|---|---|
| Membership Fees (75% refundable) | $139,900 | $199,900 | $269,900 | $339,900 | $409,900 | $479,900 |
| Annual Dues | $13,900 | $19,900 | $29,900 | $39,900 | $49,900 | $59,900 |
| **Space A** | | | | | | |
| Membership Plan | 10 day | 20 day | 30 day | 40 day | 50 day | 60 day |
| Space Available Reservation Window | 30 days | 45 days | 60 days | 75 days | 90 days | 90 days |

## Priority Holiday Access

*Peak Holiday*: Priority access for one reservation each year for the weeks that include Christmas, New Year's, Presidents' Day, or any Select Holiday week is available for a one-time fee of $59,000.

*Select Holiday*: Priority access for one reservation each year for the weeks that include Spring Break, the Fourth of July holiday, or Thanksgiving is available for a one-time fee of $39,000.

## Extended Family Sharing

Allow adult children, parents, and siblings to enjoy club benefits without a member or member spouse present for a one-time fee of $19,000 and an annual 10 percent dues premium.

**Space-Available Reservations**

For getaways on short notice, Space-Available reservations can be made at any time within the Space-Available window of the membership plan selected.

**Reservations**

A proprietary reservation network is designed to serve both the advance vacation planner and the last-minute traveler. There are two types of reservations; an Advanced Reservation and a Space-Available Reservation.

*Elite Members* may make Advanced Reservations more than ninety days in advance and Space-Available Reservations within ninety or fewer days.

*Executive Members* may make Advanced Reservations more than sixty days in advance and Space-Available Reservations within sixty or fewer days.

*Affiliate Members* may make Advanced Reservations more than forty-five days in advance and Space-Available Reservations within forty-five or fewer days.

Most destinations can be booked up to two years in advance.

**Resignation Process**

If a member chooses, Exclusive Resorts will return the entire refundable portion of the Membership fee in accordance with the terms and conditions of the Club membership Agreement. Exclusive Resorts has a 3:1 (three-in, one-out) membership resignation policy. In the history of Exclusive Resorts, there has never been a waitlist to leave the company. All Exclusive Resorts members who have decided to resign their membership have received their refund back within thirty days.

## Financial Strength

Exclusive Resorts pioneered the "Net Asset Test," the standard for financial transparency and accountability in the industry. The Net Asset Test is designed to confirm that the value of assets is sufficient to meet obligations, including repaying all refundable Membership Deposits in accordance with the terms and conditions of the Club Membership Agreement. To calculate the test, the appraised market value of the real estate holdings is added to the cash on hand, then subtracted from that amount are all secured debt and refundable Membership Deposits. Fair market value of the real estate holdings is determined by appraisals performed by an independent, nationally recognized company under generally accepted appraisal standards. There is a formal process whereby a third party conducts a full appraisal of the entire portfolio of owner real estate every two years.

Cash balances are determined by the actual cash on hand; the amount of debt includes all debt secured by the real estate assets; and refundable Membership Deposits include the total amounts refundable under the Membership Agreements should 100 percent of the members elect to resign. The consolidated financial statements reflect the findings. Exclusive Resorts has been in compliance with the Net Asset Test in 2004, 2005, 2006, and 2007.

www.exclusiveresorts.com

For Exclusive Resorts disclaimer, see footnote chapter 4/4

## Case Study #2

### Ultimate Escapes

Ultimate Escapes is a luxury destination club designed to provide individuals, families, and corporate members with flexible access to a growing portfolio of spectacular multi-million-dollar vacation residences in resort and metropolitan locations throughout the U.S., the Caribbean, Mexico, and Europe. In addition to staying in beautifully appointed homes in the most desirable vacation settings, members enjoy five-star concierge services and the amenities of a luxury resort or hotel.

### The Residences

Each Ultimate Escapes residence welcomes you with a host of wonderful club amenities. Enjoy all the comforts of home, including fully equipped chef's kitchens, king-size beds with luxury linens, wine cellars stocked with favorite vintages, spa-inspired bathrooms, plasma TVs, WiFi connectivity, video game entertainment centers, and integrated audio and surround stereo. Depending on their location, some homes also feature swimming pools, hot tubs, fireplaces, and multiple terraces and/or decks.

### Service

The Member Services team and 24/7 on-site concierge offer a level of personalized attention that elevates each holiday to the sublime.

Vacations are planned from beginning to end by an experienced travel professional assisting with travel arrangements and airport transfers. Once you're on site, the concierge can make reservations for activities, stock the refrigerator with requested groceries and assist with every detail including procuring the services of a butler, nanny or private chef.

The concierge can also provide access to exclusive beach and swim clubs, golf courses, health clubs, spas and private country clubs to the member for enjoyment of all resort-style amenities.

## The Ultimate Collection <sup>SM</sup> Luxury Hotels

### North America & Mexico
Boston, MA
Ft. Lauderdale, FL
Guintana Roo, Mexico
Minneapolis, MN
Orlando, FL
Puerto Vallarta, Mexico
Punta Mita, Mexico

### Europe
Algarve, Portugal
Amsterdam, Netherlands
Barcelona, Spain
Brussels, Belgium
Copenhagen, Denmark
Dublin, Ireland
Frankfurt, Germany
Geneva, Switzerland
Genoa, Italy
Hamburg, Germany

Innsbruck, Austria
Lisbon, Portugal
London, England
Lucerne, Switzerland
Madrid, Spain
Milan, Italy
Monte Carlo, Monaco
Munich, Germany
Naples, Italy
Oslo, Norway
Paris, France
Prague, Czech Republic
Rome, Italy
Stockholm, Sweden
St. Petersburg, Russia

**Central & South America**
Bogota, Columbia
Buenos Aires, Argentina
Roatan, Honduras

**Middle East & Africa**
Bahrain
Brunei
Delhi, India
Dubai, United Arab Emirates
Kuwait
Mumbai, India
Nairobi, Kenya
Riyadh, Saudi Arabia
Tel Aviv, Israel

**Asia & Australia**

Beijing, China
Bali, Indonesia
Brisbane, Australia
Guangzhou, China
Hanoi, Vietnam
Ho Chi Minh City, Vietnam
Hong Kong, China
Jakarta, Indonesia
Kuala Lumpur, Malaysia
Macau, China
Maldives
Melbourne, Australia
Osaka, Japan
Seoul, Korea
Singapore
Shanghai, China
Sydney, Australia
Taipai, Taiwan
Tokyo, Japan
Xiamen, China

**Ultimate Escapes Club Destinations**
**130 Homes Available in Over 40 Destinations**

Abaco, Bahamas
Anguilla*
Barbados*
Beaver Creek, CO
Belize
Bend, Oregon

Big Island, Hawaii
British Virgin Islands*
Cabo San Lucas, Mexico
Cap Cana, DR
Candlewood Lake, CT
Chicago, IL
Copper Mountain, CO
Deer Valley, UT
Fox Acres, CO
Ft. Lauderdale, FL*
Grand Cayman Islands*
Indian Rocks Beach, FL
Jackson Hole, WY
Kiawah, SC
Key West, FL
La Buscadora, BVI
La Costa, CA
La Quinta, CA
Lake George, NY
Lake Las Vegas, NV
London, England
Maui, HI
Miami Beach, FL
Napa, CA*
Naples, FL
Nevis, West Indies
New York City, NY
Outerbanks, NC
Orlando, FL
Palm Beach, FL

Paris, France
Punta Cana, DR
Punta Mita, Mexico
Reserva Conchal, Costa Rica
Reynolds Plantation, GA
Rome, Italy*
San Diego, CA*
San Francisco, CA*
Scottsdale, AZ
St, John, USVI
Stowe, VT
Sun Valley, ID
Telluride, CO
Tuscany, Italy
Vail, CO
Watercolor, FL

*Planned Destinations

## Membership Plans

The key distinction in the membership plans is the different real estate value of each of the club's homes. Ultimate Escapes Premiere Club℠ residences have an average value of $1 million. Ultimate Escapes Signature Club℠ residences have an average value of $2 million, and Ultimate Escapes Elite Club℠ residences have an average value of $3 million.

# Ultimate Escapes Premiere Club[SM]

## Family Plans                                              $1 million home values

|  | Platinum Plus | Platinum | Gold | Silver | Bronze |
|---|---|---|---|---|---|
| Membership Fee | $150,000 | $115,000 | $105,000 | $95,000 | $70,000 |
| Included Days | 60 | 42 | 28 | 21 | 14 |
| Advance Reservations | 5 | 4 | 3 | 2 | 1 |
| Advance Holiday Reservations | 2 | 2 | 1 | 1 | 1** |
| Space A | Inside 180 Days | Inside 150 Days | Inside 120 Days | Inside 90 Days | Inside 90 Days |
| Annual Dues | $17,000 | $12,000 | $11,000 | $9,500 | $8,000 |

**Bronze Members Serve (one) Holiday Advanced Reservation Every Other Year.

# Ultimate Escapes Signature Club[SM]

## Family Plans                                              $2 million home values

|  | Platinum Plus | Platinum | Gold | Silver | Bronze |
|---|---|---|---|---|---|
| Membership Fee | $300,000 | $240,000 | $215,000 | $195,000 | $145,000 |
| Included Days | 60 | 42 | 28 | 21 | 14 |
| Advance Reservations | 5 | 4 | 3 | 2 | 1 |
| Advance Holiday Reservations | 2 | 2 | 1 | 1 | 1** |
| Space A | Inside 180 Days | Inside 180 Days | Inside 150 Days | Inside 120 Days | Inside 90 Days |
| Annual Dues | $35,500 | $25,000 | $18,500 | $15,500 | $11,500 |

**Bronze Members Serve (one) Holiday Advanced Reservation Every Other Year.

# Ultimate Escapes Elite Club<sup>SM</sup>

| Family Plans | | | | | $3 million home values |
| --- | --- | --- | --- | --- | --- |
| | Platinum Plus | Platinum | Gold | Silver | Bronze |
| Membership Fee | $450,000 | $375,000 | $355,000 | $275,000 | $200,000 |
| Included Days | 60 | 42 | 28 | 21 | 14 |
| Advance Reservations | 5 | 4 | 3 | 2 | 1 |
| Advance Holiday Reservations | 2 | 2 | 1 | 1 | 1** |
| Space A | Inside 180 Days | Inside 180 Days | Inside 150 Days | Inside 120 Days | Inside 90 Days |
| Annual Dues | $49,000 | $35,500 | $27,500 | $23,000 | $16,000 |

**Bronze Members Serve (one) Holiday Advanced Reservation Every Other Year.

## Equivalent Member-to-Property Ratio: 6:1

## Resignation Policy

Members of Ultimate Escapes acquire a lifetime membership. Should any member decide to leave the Club, Ultimate Escapes will redeem membership at 80 percent of the then-current membership price. Ultimate Escapes operate on a three-in, one-out resignation policy (3:1), and any resigning member will receive the entire refundable portion as detailed in the terms and conditions of the Club Membership Agreement.

### Financial Strength

The lifetime Membership comes with a Membership Warranty that guarantees all members' deposits by placing the properties in a Member Trust. The Membership Warranty is unique in the industry and sets a high standard of security. As well, the growing real estate portfolio ensures that sufficient assets meet any debt obligation, including refunding membership fees in accordance with the Club Membership Agreement. The lifetime Membership is backed by real estate and financial expertise of a management team with a rock-solid track record with leading financial and real estate companies.

www.ultimateescapes.com
For Ultimate Escapes disclaimer see footnote chapter 4/5

## Discovery Model Applied to Exclusive Resorts and Ultimate Escapes

| | EXCLUSIVE RESORTS | ULTIMATE ESCAPES |
|---|---|---|
| **A USE RIGHT** | 10, 20, 30, 40, 50, 60 day | 14, 21, 28, 42, 60 day |
| **B USE SYSTEM** | Membership applicaion | Membership application |
| | Membership agreement | Membership agreement |
| Resignation Process in accordance with terms and conditions | 3:1 | 3:1 |
| | 75 % refundable deposit | 80% refundable deposit |
| Membership Tenure | 30 years (transferable) | Lifetime (transferable) |
| Finacial Strength | Net Asset Test | Membership Warranty |
| | | Net Asset Test |
| Membership Dues | Yes | Yes |

### C USE MANAGEMENT PLANS

| | EXCLUSIVE RESORTS | ULTIMATE ESCAPES |
|---|---|---|
| Membership Plans | Elite | Platinum Plus (60 days) |
| | Executive | Platinum (42 days) |
| | Affiliate | Gold (28 days) |
| | | Silver (21 days) |
| | | Bronze (14 days) |
| Reservations | Advance reservations | Advance reservations |
| | Space-available | Advance holiday |
| | Fee based: Priorit Holiday | Space-available |
| | Access and Extended | |
| | Family Sharing Plans | |
| Programs | 'Once in a Lifetime' | Ultimate Collection |
| | Planned annual events | Planned annual events |
| | Guest privileges | Guest privileges |
| | Membership | Membership |
| | transferability | transferability |
| Services | 24/7 on-site concierge | 24/7 on-site concierge |
| | Vacation planning | Vacation planning |
| | Pre-arrival provisioning | Pre-arrival provisioning |
| | Privileded access to | Privileded access to |
| | Resort amenities | Resort amenities |
| Member to Property Ratio | 7:1 | 6:1 |

## Summary

From these two examples, it is easy to see how each club has devised a unique use right and management plan. There are many clubs to explore, and if this shared-use offering intrigues you, it's in your interest to investigate all the clubs. Each club has its own Web site, and I would encourage you to visit all the club sites. One of the more comprehensive independent Web sites that keeps current on the destination club industry, providing comparison charts and fees, is www.sherpareport.com.

The Crittenden Report is an independent industry resource publication on news and analysis covering the real estate industry. The Crittenden Resort Report includes news and analysis on the resort real estate industry, including destination clubs. www.crittendonreport.com

## Some Questions to Consider:

*Lifestyle:*
- ❑ How many days a year do you vacation? This will help you decide on the membership plan that best fits your use needs. Do you need to include extra days for an extended family plan?
- ❑ Do you travel at peak times every year or are you fairly flexible?
- ❑ What types of homes do you want to stay in when you vacation? Clubs can sometimes differentiate membership levels by the price of residences.
- ❑ What plan offers you the places you want to go?
- ❑ What level of service are you looking for before you go, while you're on vacation and after you return?

❏ What type of accommodations does the club have, in the places you presently vacation?

❏ What is the member-to-residence ratio of the club?

❏ What are the process and fees for upgrading within the club?

❏ Always ask about the little things that are relevant to your family that could make a difference in the vacation experience. Does the concierge service book everything for you, like swimming lessons for your son or a birthday cake for your daughter, or is the service more basic? Are there any pet-friendly destinations? How many residences can accommodate your extended family of fifteen or a reunion? How many are small enough for romantic getaways for just two? Are there enough amenities in each home to amuse your children? Remember, the investment can be substantial, and it is always the little things that weren't big enough to ask about that can make all the difference in which club you'll decide to join.

## *Clubs:*

❏ Does the club have the style of accommodations you require in the destinations you want to vacation in?

❏ Does the club offer the types of services you might enjoy?

❏ Does the club offer "experiential" vacation opportunities? Would those types of vacations enhance membership or not?

❏ Are the club fees appropriate for your travel and vacation patterns?

❏ How long has the club been operating? What is its operational history?

- Who is the management team?
- What is the current club member satisfaction level?
- How does the club communicate with its members?
- What is the growth/business model for the club?
- What financial securities are in place for your membership deposit?
- What financial statements are available to you on an annual basis?
- What is the resignation policy, in terms of deposit refund and "in-out" ratio?
- Does the reservation procedure fit your travel patterns?
- Does the club offer perpetual membership or is there a term limit on membership?
- What is the annual dues policy? When and how much can it increase?
- Is the club an equity or non-equity club?

# Final Notes

*"If our lives are dominated by a search for happiness, then perhaps few activities reveal as much about the dynamics of this quest ... as our travels. They express, however inarticulately, an understanding of what life might be about, outside of the constraints of work and of the struggle for survival."*

Alain De Botton, *The Art of Travel*

In my youth, vacations were something that happened during the summer holidays. The anticipation was almost unbearable as May and June came around the calendar corner and we went into the home stretch. But I grew up in a much simpler time, where stay-at-home moms were the norm, dads worked a nine-to-five job, and vacations happened when school was out.

Today, for most families, vacations are almost a necessity to reconnect and simply have some fun away from the stresses of busy, fast-paced lives. Families now get away during Presidents' Week and spring break, short ski weekends, and beach holidays throughout the year. They fly, they drive and they cruise. If I had wanted to see a gorilla when I was young, my mother would have taken me to the zoo. Today, families can see gorillas in the wild, in any number of trekking vacations the industry offers.

One of the benefits of shared ownership/use is the commitment a family makes to take the time, at least once every year and for those extremely fortunate ones many times a year to share experiences, stack the family photo albums, and build extraordinary memories with their loved ones.

Timeshare, or vacation ownership, is now part of the American lexicon. Over four million American families now enjoy the finest resorts around the world, and that number will continue to grow as families discover the flexibility and value of the industry.

Fractionals and private residence clubs continue to appeal to families who have discovered a special place that renews their spirits and their connection to each other. Destination clubs will continue to provide extraordinary destinations and residences for affluent families who want the adventure of travel and who want to experience it in different places in remarkable accommodations.

The shared ownership/use industry is still in its infancy and will continue to adapt and reinvent itself. But the foundations explored in the Discovery Model should be a useful guide for many years to come, as you explore the industry and perhaps join the millions of families who were trailblazers.

# Glossary

**Amenities:** Desirable features in a resort or property that add value to the vacationing experience. Amenities include swimming pools, fitness facilities, golf, boating, and planned activities. Some amenities like spa services, golf, and water sport equipment may carry an additional charge.

**American Resort Development Association (ARDA):** The professional association representing the vacation ownership and resort development industries. Members range from privately held companies to publicly traded companies and international corporations with expertise in shared ownership interests in leisure real estate. The membership also includes timeshare owners associations (HOAs), resort management companies, and consumer owners through the ARDA Resort Owners Coalition (ARDA-ROC). ARDA has a Code of Ethics that defines key elements of the vacation ownership and community development business and outlines appropriate practices that each individual and member company is required to follow. Read more at www.ARDA.org and the new consumer Web site at www.VacationBetter.org

**Banking:** Depositing a week(s) of timeshare into an exchange system or inventory pool.

**Biennial or Biannual:** Use every other year.

**Bonus Weeks**: A timeshare term used to describe an offering where resort, exchange companies, or developers offer members additional use right (with low rental fees) without members relinquishing any use right in return.

**Closing Costs:** Expenses paid by the buyer and/or seller at the time of closing a real estate transaction.

**Developer:** The company responsible for constructing and selling and in many cases, managing the resort.

**Deed:** A legal document used to convey an interest in real property, where the title of the real property transfers from one party to another.

**Destination Club:**
*Non-equity clubs* – A new luxury vacation alternative based on a country club model, where members join a private club, and pay an initial membership fee and annual dues in return for access to a changing inventory of luxury accommodations and service programs. Club developers retain ownership or have the use rights in the real estate portfolio. A deposit refund mechanism is typical in most clubs. This is by far the most prevalent type of club offered.
*Equity clubs* – Members own a share in the limited liability company/partnership that owns the clubs and/or its properties. Since shares are issued and members receive registered securities, clubs need to comply with security laws.

**Exchange:** A system that is designed to accommodate the trade of use rights for different accommodation and/or travel-related services. External exchange companies provide this service to resort partners. An internal exchange mechanism is offered in many companies that can allow exchange within the resort group. Exchange programs can be offered for timeshare, fractional, and private residence clubs and may be fee related.

**Fixed Ownership:** A type of timeshare, fractional, and private residence club ownership in which the owner knows the specific use rights within a given year in which he has access.

**Floating Ownership:** A type of timeshare ownership where the use rights are subject to the owner reserving the week within the season purchased, typically on a first-come, first-served basis.

**Fractionals/Private Residence Clubs:** Luxury resort real estate with related use rights in increments from two weeks to twelve weeks. Often referred to as "shares," this type of real estate is almost always deeded, provides a high level of service and amenities, and is considered the luxury tier of shared ownership. Fractionals and private residence clubs are regulated under most state timeshare acts, rules, and/or laws.

**Homeowners Association (HOA):** An association of all owners of a particular property designed to manage, operate, and administer the development. An elected board of directors made up of homeowners typically directs the management, but typically a professional management company is hired to run the day-to-day operations. For timeshare developments, in most cases, the resort developer will be the property manager.

**Home Resort:** A timeshare term used to designate the resort location of where the use right is.

**Maintenance Fee:** Also called HOA dues or fees, annual assessment, or annual dues. This is an annual fee owners are required to pay to cover the cost of running the resort, daily and long term upkeep, improvements, staff requirements, common area utilities, and so on. Timeshare, fractional interest, and destination clubs require this fee.

**Member-to-Property Ratio:** A term used in destination clubs to describe the ratio between members and accommodations in the real estate portfolio. Typically a 6:1 ratio means there are six members for one accommodation. The ratio fluctuates as accommodations and members are increased or decreased, but clubs strive to maintain a certain member-to-property ratio.

**Points:** A symbolic measurement of value used in the management plan of some resort developments. Use rights are relinquished for a "currency" called points or credits. Resort accommodation are assigned a point value based on unit size, length of stay, location, season, and what travel-related services may be offered. Owners then spend their points to reserve accommodation/services based on their estimated vacation needs. The points system is used by some companies for both internal and external exchanges.

**Private Residence Club:** See Fractional/Private Residence Club.

**Rescission:** The period of time granted under state law during which a purchaser can cancel the purchase contract without penalty and receive a complete and full refund of all monies paid to the seller. Dictated by state statute and company policy, timeshare rescission periods vary from state to state, but range from three to ten days, the most common being five days. This applies to timeshare, fractional, and private residence clubs.

**Resignation System:** Refers to the non-equity destination clubs where a refund mechanism is in place for those members wishing to resign from the club; they receive a partial refund of their membership deposit after certain conditions are met.

**Right-to-Use:** The buyer has the right to use the unit for a specified number of years. At the end of that period, the use rights return back to the property owner, who continually owns the underlying title. The buyer can usually sell, donate, or bequeath a right-to-use contract, but the expiration date will remain the same.

**Timeshare:** A prepaid use right for less than a year for multiple years in a vacation accommodation or leisure real estate property.

## Resources, References and Endnotes

There are so many articles, Web sites and documents on the shared ownership/use industry that it is not possible to write a book without drawing from some of these myriad sources. They include, but are not limited to:

Vacation Ownership Guide by the American Resort Developers Association www.ARDA.org

Timeshare Beat – www.timesharebeat.com

Sherpa Report – www.sherpareport.com

Helium Report – www.heliumreport.com

Halogen Guides – www.halogenguides.com

Ragatz Associates – www.ragatzassociates.com

# Footnotes

## Introduction

1. Expedia.com: Seventh Annual Vacation Deprivation Survey
2. ARDA International Foundation (AIF): State of the Vacation Timeshare Industry, United States Study, 2006 edition
3. Personal Interview with Leaf Van Boven, PhD

## Chapter 1

1. Eilene Zimmerman. "If One Vacation Home Won't Do, How About A Bunch?" (Money and Business/Financial Desk)(Spending), *New York Times*, July 1, 2007
2. *Wall Street Journal* (12-29-07) www.wallstreetjournal
3. ARDA International Foundation (AIF): State of The Vacation Timeshare Industry, United States Study, 2006 edition
4. ARDA "Understanding Vacation Ownership" To view or download a copy, go the ARDA Web site (www.arda.org), then click on "Consumer Information".
5. www.thetimesharebeat.com
6. Personal interview with Robert Webb

## Chapter 2

1. ARDA International Foundation (AIF): State of the Vacation Industry, United States Study, 2008 edition
2. Personal interview with Carl Berry

3./4./5. ARDA International Foundation (AIF): State of the Vacation Timeshare Industry: United States Study, 2008 edition

6. Hyatt Vacation Club Disclosure: Hyatt Hotels Corporation, Hyatt Vacation Ownership, Inc., their officers, directors, partners and all affiliates, subsidiaries, and parent companies as well as the parent company and all affiliates and subsidiaries of their affiliates, subsidiaries and parent companies, make no warranty, express or implied, as to the condition, capacity, performance or any other aspect of the Hyatt Vacation Club or other activities, events or service providers described in this publication. No inquiry has been made into the activities or events, or the qualifications or the quality of service offered by the providers. Do not consider the inclusion of materials relating to the Hyatt Vacation Club or this disclosure as an endorsement or recommendation of the Hyatt Vacation Club or for any of the activities, events or providers. Membership in the Hyatt Vacation Club is subject to the terms and conditions set forth in the Hyatt Vacation Club Rules and Regulations and the Multi-Site Public Offering Statement of the Hyatt Vacation Club, which are subject to change.

7. Intrawest: All prices, programs, services and amenities are subject to change at any time.

## Chapter 3

1./2./3. Ragatz Associates, State of the Shared Ownership/ Use Industry Report, 2007

4. The Hammocks at Bald Head Island: The developer reserves the right to change prices, programs, services and amenities at any time.

5. The Cottages at Cape Kiwanda: The developer reserves the right to change prices, programs, services and amenities at any time.

6./7. Ragatz Associates, State of the Shared Ownership/Use Industry Report, 2007

8. The Ritz-Carlton Club and Residences, Kapalua Bay disclaimer:

   Prices are tentative and subject to change. Services and amenities are proposed only. Kapalua memberships are subject to terms and conditions. All memberships to all programs are subject to The Ritz-Carlton Membership Program Reservation Procedures and Policies and the Multi-site Public Offering Statement of The Ritz-Carlton Club.

   Kapalua Bay, LLC., and The Ritz-Carlton Development Company, Inc., their officers, directors, partners and all affiliates, subsidiaries and parent companies, as well as the parent company and all affiliates and subsidiaries of their affiliates, subsidiaries and parent companies, make no warranty, express or implied, as to the condition, capacity, performance or any other aspect of the activities, events or service providers listed herein. No inquiry has been made into the activities or events, or the qualifications or the quality of service offered by the providers. Do not consider this an endorsement of or recommendation for any of the activities, events or providers.

   The Residences at Kapalua Bay and The Ritz-Carlton Club, Kapalua Bay are not owned or developed by The Ritz-Carlton Hotel Company, LLC. An affiliate of the Ritz-Carlton Hotel Company, LLC., owns an interest in

Kapalua Bay, LLC., the developer, and The Residences at Kapalua Bay will be managed by The Ritz-Carlton Hotel Company, LLC., Kapalua Bay, LLC., uses the Ritz-Carlton trademarks under license from The Ritz-Carlton Hotel Company, LLC., which may be terminated or revoked according to its terms.

9. Meriwether Ranch disclaimer: Prices and programs and offerings are subject to change at any time.
10. Ragatz Associates, State of the Shared ownership/use Industry report, 2007

## Chapter 4

1. Ragatz Associates, State of the Shared Ownership/Use Industry 2007 edition
2. Sherpa Report www.sherpareport.com
3. Adam Wegner, personal interview
4. Exclusive Resorts Disclaimer: Prices and programs and offerings are subject to change at any time.
5. Ultimate Escapes Disclaimer: Prices and programs and offerings are subject to change at any time.

## About the Author

Elaine Joli, an expert in real estate marketing, has been working with top developers in Canada and the United States for more than sixteen years. She was the marketing consultant to one of the largest ski resort developers in North America, developed and directed marketing strategies for one of the largest master planned communities in the United States, and has helped dozens of developers sell millions of dollars in resort real estate. Her experience also includes working with the largest timeshare sales training company in the world. Her campaigns have won industry awards, and she continues to enjoy working in the industry.